Sexuality and Gender

Series Editor: Cara Acred

Volume 297

Independer

First published by Independence Educational Publishers

The Studio, High Green

Great Shelford

Cambridge CB22 5EG

England

© Independence 2016

ISBN-13: 978 1 86168 738 8

Printed in Great Britain
Zenith Print Group

Contents

Introduction

Sexuality and Gender is Volume 297 in the **ISSUES** series. The aim of the series is to offer current, diverse information about important issues in our world, from a UK perspective.

ABOUT SEXUALITY AND GENDER

Did you know that one in two young people say they are not 100% heterosexual? With so many labels now used to define sexuality and gender identity, this book will help guide you in understanding sexuality and gender, plus other LGBTQ+ issues. Exploring terms from asexuality and non-binary to transgender and intersex, this book also discusses topics such as gender dysphoria, mental health and LGBT representation in the media, as well as challenging homophobic language, transgender bathroom rights and legal equality for all.

OUR SOURCES

Titles in the **ISSUES** series are designed to function as educational resource books, providing a balanced overview of a specific subject.

The information in our books is comprised of facts, articles and opinions from many different sources, including:

⇨ Newspaper reports and opinion pieces

⇨ Website factsheets

⇨ Magazine and journal articles

⇨ Statistics and surveys

⇨ Government reports

⇨ Literature from special interest groups.

A NOTE ON CRITICAL EVALUATION

Because the information reprinted here is from a number of different sources, readers should bear in mind the origin of the text and whether the source is likely to have a particular bias when presenting information (or when conducting their research). It is hoped that, as you read about the many aspects of the issues explored in this book, you will critically evaluate the information presented.

It is important that you decide whether you are being presented with facts or opinions. Does the writer give a biased or unbiased report? If an opinion is being expressed, do you agree with the writer? Is there potential bias to the 'facts' or statistics behind an article?

ASSIGNMENTS

In the back of this book, you will find a selection of assignments designed to help you engage with the articles you have been reading and to explore your own opinions. Some tasks will take longer than others and there is a mixture of design, writing and research-based activities that you can complete alone or in a group.

FURTHER RESEARCH

At the end of each article we have listed its source and a website that you can visit if you would like to conduct your own research. Please remember to critically evaluate any sources that you consult and consider whether the information you are viewing is accurate and unbiased.

Useful weblinks

www.actionfortranshealth.org.uk

www.channel4.com/news

www.ditchthelabel.org

www.each.education

www.glaad.org

www.huffingtonpost.co.uk

www.independent.co.uk

www.leapsports.org

www.lgbtyouth.org.uk

www.newfamilysocial.org.uk

www.nhs.uk

www.ohchr.org

www.onepoll.com

www.PeterTatchellFoundation.org

www.stonewall.org.uk

www.theconversation.com

www.theguardian.com

www.transmediawatch.org

www.unfe.org

www.yougov.co.uk

www.young.scot

www.youngstonewall.org.uk

LGBT rights

Frequently asked questions.

What does 'LGBT' mean?

LGBT stands for 'lesbian, gay, bisexual and transgender'. While these terms have increasing global resonance, in different cultures other terms may be used to describe people who form same-sex relationships and those who exhibit non-binary gender identities (such as hijra, meti, lala, skesana, motsoalle, mithli, kuchu, kawein, travesty, muxé, fa'afafine, fakaleiti, hamjensgara and Two-Spirit). In a human rights context, lesbian, gay, bisexual and transgender people face both common and distinct challenges. Intersex people (those born with atypical sex characteristics) suffer many of the same kinds of human rights violations as LGBT people, as indicated below.

What is 'sexual orientation'?

Sexual orientation refers to a person's physical, romantic and/or emotional attraction towards other people. Everyone has a sexual orientation, which is integral to a person's identity. Gay men and lesbian women are attracted to individuals of the same sex as themselves. Heterosexual people (sometimes known as 'straight') are attracted to individuals of a different sex from themselves. Bisexual people may be attracted to individuals of the same or different sex. Sexual orientation is not related to gender identity.

What is 'gender identity'?

Gender identity reflects a deeply felt and experienced sense of one's own gender. A person's gender identity is typically consistent with the sex assigned to them at birth. For transgender people, there is an inconsistency between their sense of their own gender and the sex they were assigned at birth. In some cases, their appearance and mannerisms and other outwards characteristics may conflict with society's expectations of gender-normative behaviour.

What does transgender mean?

Transgender (sometimes shortened to "trans") is an umbrella term used to describe a wide range of identities – including transsexual people, cross-dressers (sometimes referred to as "transvestites"), people who identify as third gender, and others whose appearance and characteristics are perceived as gender atypical. Transwomen identify as women but were classified as males when they were born. Transmen identify as men but were classified female when they were born. Some transgender

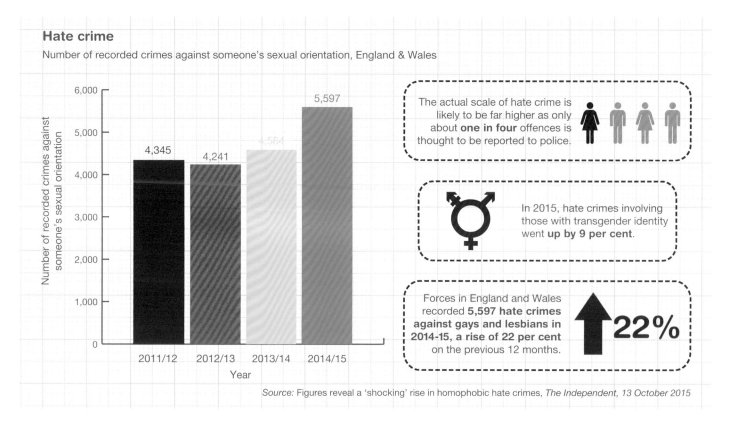

Hate crime

Number of recorded crimes against someone's sexual orientation, England & Wales

The actual scale of hate crime is likely to be far higher as only about **one in four** offences is thought to be reported to police.

In 2015, hate crimes involving those with transgender identity went **up by 9 per cent**.

Forces in England and Wales recorded **5,597 hate crimes against gays and lesbians in 2014-15, a rise of 22 per cent** on the previous 12 months.

22%

Source: Figures reveal a 'shocking' rise in homophobic hate crimes, *The Independent*, 13 October 2015

people seek surgery or take hormones to bring their body into alignment with their gender identity; others do not.

What is intersex?

An intersex person is born with sexual anatomy, reproductive organs and/or chromosome patterns that do not fit the typical definition of male or female. This may be apparent at birth or become so later in life. An intersex person may identify as male or female or as neither. Intersex status is not about sexual orientation or gender identity: intersex people experience the same range of sexual orientations and gender identities as non-intersex people.

What are homophobia and transphobia?

Homophobia is an irrational fear of, hatred or aversion towards lesbian, gay or bisexual people; transphobia denotes an irrational fear, hatred or aversion towards transgender people. Because the term homophobia is widely understood, it is often used in an all-encompassing way to refer to fear, hatred and aversion towards LGBT people in general.

What kind of human rights violations are LGBT people exposed to?

LGBT people of all ages and in all regions of the world suffer from violations of their human rights. They are physically attacked, kidnapped, raped and murdered. In more than a third of the world's countries, people may be arrested and jailed (and in at least five countries executed) for engaging in private, consensual, same-sex relationships. States often fail to adequately protect LGBT people from discriminatory treatment in the private sphere, including in the workplace, housing and healthcare. LGBT children and adolescents face bullying in school and may be thrown out of their homes by their parents, forced into psychiatric institutions or forced to marry. Transgender people are often denied identity papers that reflect their preferred gender, without which they cannot work, travel, open a bank account or access services. Intersex children may be subjected to surgical and other interventions without their or often their parents' informed consent, and as adults are also vulnerable to violence and discrimination.

Is there any reason to criminalise homosexuality?

No. Criminalising private sexual relationships between consenting adults, whether the relationships are same-sex or different-sex, is a violation of the right to privacy. Laws criminalising consensual same-sex relationships are also discriminatory, and where enforced, violate rights to freedom from arbitrary arrest and detention. At least 76 countries have laws in effect that criminalise private, consensual same-sex relationships, and in at least five countries conviction may carry the death penalty. In addition to violating basic rights, this criminalisation serves to legitimise hostile attitudes towards LGBT people, feeding violence and discrimination. It also hampers efforts to halt the spread of HIV by deterring LGBT people from coming forward for testing and treatment for fear of revealing criminal activity.

Are there LGBT people only in Western countries?

No. LGBT people exist everywhere, in all countries, among all ethnic groups, at all socioeconomic levels and in all communities. Claims that same-sex attraction is a western practice are false. However, many of the criminal laws used today to punish LGBT people are Western in origin. In most cases, they were imposed on the countries concerned in the 19th century by the colonial powers of the day.

Have LGBT people always existed?

Yes. LGBT people have always been a part of our communities. There are examples from every locality and time-period, from prehistoric rock paintings in South Africa and Egypt to ancient Indian medical texts and early Ottoman literature. Many societies have traditionally been open towards LGBT people, including several Asian societies that have traditionally recognised a third gender.

Is it possible to change a person's sexual orientation and gender identity?

No. A person's sexual orientation and/or gender identity cannot be changed. What must change are the negative social attitudes that stigmatise LGBT people and contribute to violence and discrimination against them. Attempts to change someone's sexual orientation often involve human rights violations and can cause severe trauma. Examples include forced psychiatric therapies intended to 'cure' (sic) individuals of their same-sex attraction, as well as the so-called 'corrective' rape of lesbians perpetrated with the declared aim of 'turning them straight'.

Does being around LGBT people or having access to information on homosexuality endanger the well-being of children?

No. Learning about or spending time with people who are LGBT does not influence the sexual orientation or gender identity of minors nor can it harm their well-being. Rather, it is vital that all youth have access to age-appropriate sexuality education to ensure that they have healthy, respectful physical relationships and can protect themselves from sexually transmitted infections. Denial of this kind of information contributes to stigma and can cause young LGBT people to feel isolated, depressed, forcing some to drop out of school and contributing to higher rates of suicide.

Are gay, lesbian, bisexual or transgender people dangerous to children?

No. There is no link between homosexuality and child abuse of any kind. LGBT people all over the world can be good parents, teachers and role models for young people. Portraying LGBT people as 'paedophiles' or dangerous to children is wholly inaccurate, offensive and a distraction from the need for serious and appropriate measures to protect all children, including those coming to terms with their sexual orientation and gender identity.

Does international human rights law apply to LGBT people?

Yes, it applies to every person. International human rights law establishes legal obligations on states to make sure that everyone, without distinction, can enjoy their human rights. A person's sexual orientation and gender identity is a status, like race, sex, colour or religion. United Nations human rights experts have confirmed that international law prohibits discrimination based on sexual orientation or gender identity.

Can depriving LGBT people of their human rights be justified on grounds of religion, culture or tradition?

No. Human rights are universal: every human being is entitled to the same rights, no matter who they are or where they live. While history, culture and religion are contextually important, all states, regardless of their political, economic and cultural systems, have a legal duty to promote and protect the human rights of all.

⇨ The above information is reprinted with kind permission from Free & Equal and the Office of the High Commissioner for Human Rights (OHCHR). Please visit www.unfe.org and www.ohchr.org for more information.

Am I LGBT?

Questioning your sexual orientation can be difficult, often because of other people's attitudes. But it could make perfect sense of feelings you've had for a long time.

Whether you're straight, lesbian, gay, bisexual or transgender, there's no reason not to feel confident and proud of who you are.

I keep hearing this word 'sexuality' – what is it?

Sexuality isn't just about sex, it's about your feelings, emotions, attractions and desires and how you express these.

It includes whether we're attracted to women, men or both (our sexual orientation) and what we do sexually.

Having sexual thoughts and feelings is a normal, healthy part of human life. This is true whether you're attracted to men, women or both. Some people aren't much interested in sex at all, and this is normal too.

When will I know if I'm gay or straight or bisexual or transgender?

It takes time to figure out who we are sexually and to understand our gender identity and orientation, just as it takes time to figure out other areas of our lives.

The important thing is to be true to how you feel at the time and to respect yourself and others around you.

So-and-so knows me really well and reckons I'm gay/lesbian/bisexual/transgender – am I?

It's true that good friends can sometimes tell us things about ourselves we might not have realised, but you shouldn't be swayed too much by what anyone else says about your sexuality.

Only you know can how you really feel inside.

If I think I am gay, lesbian, bisexual or transgender – should I tell people?

We have a guide on coming out as gay, lesbian or bisexual, as well as a guide on how to come out as transgender. There are many different things you should take into consideration when it comes to coming out, but it's entirely your decision.

I had a sex dream about someone who's the same sex as me – what does it mean?

Having one dream about a same-sex mate probably doesn't mean you're gay or lesbian.

On the other hand, if your sexy dreams are always about members of your own sex, and you enjoy similar fantasies and daydreams, they could be telling you something.

I suddenly thought about someone my own sex while I was masturbating – what does it mean?

For lots of us, sexuality isn't as simple as being gay or lesbian or straight. Lots of people have fantasies involving people the same sex as them, even if they wouldn't want to actually have sex with them.

Meanwhile, if your sexual fantasies are usually about people of your own sex and have been for a while, it's a pretty strong indication you're attracted to people the same sex as you.

Me and my mate started getting off with each other – am I gay/lesbian?

Having a sexual experience with someone the same sex as you does not make you gay or lesbian.

Three things here:
1. It's normal to feel physically attracted sometimes to people we're close to.
2. Hormones surge during puberty.
3. Lots of people end up experimenting sexually with their same-sex mates.

In answer to the question, only time will tell. You might become life-long lovers, or one or both of you both might feel completely different about each other as time passes. You might decide to pursue other same-sex relationships or you might not.

In the meantime, you should know that what happened is a fairly normal part of growing up and try not to stress about it.

What if I feel I'm really a different sex and am in the wrong body?

The term 'transgender' describes a range of people whose feelings about their gender identity (who they feel they are) differ from the assumptions made about them when they were born.

Transgender people can be attracted to men, women, both or neither, regardless of their sex at birth or the gender they choose to live as.

Some transgender people choose to live as their birth sex, some as the gender they feel they really are. Others may decide to be open about being transgender with some people but not with everyone.

More info

Check out the LGBT Youth Scotland website: www.lgbtyouth.org.uk.

You can also get advice via mobile phone from LGBT Youth Scotland by texting 'info' and where you are in Scotland to 0778 148 17 88.

⇨ The above information is reprinted with kind permission from Young Scot. Please visit www.young.scot for more information.

© Young Scot

Disclaimer: Sexuality and gender identity are often talked about together but they are separate from one another.

Bisexual

What does 'bisexual' mean?

The word bisexual describes a person who is attracted to both men and women.

It is normal to question your sexuality and part of growing up is discovering and learning about yourself. It is also normal to have feelings towards other people, both men and women.

Am I old enough to know?

Everyone is different and there is no right or wrong age to realise you are bisexual. Sexuality can be fluid and you may be attracted to different people at different times in your life.

Young people are often told that they don't know themselves well enough or should wait until they are older before they decide. Many young men say they have known for a long time that they feel 'different' to others and they are aware of their attraction to both men and women at a young age. It's OK to feel like this and it is OK to change your mind. Sexuality does not need to be fixed forever – for some people it will be, and for others it might shift over time.

What do bisexual people look like?

There is often a myth that bisexual people are either lesbian or gay men who have not yet decided. This is untrue and bisexual people have the right to be attracted to both men and women without needing to choose one. Straight people are not defined just by who they are attracted to, so there is no reason why you should be. Stereotypes don't really define any individual; we are much too diverse for that! You can be exactly the person you want to be and should never feel pressure to act or look a certain way.

Is it normal?

There are still some messages out there that make us believe that it is not OK or normal to be attracted to both men and women. Some societies and communities do not accept this difference. It is completely normal to have feelings for both men and women and we can offer support and advice to help you feel more comfortable about who you are.

Some useful info

Bisexual – A person who is emotionally and/or physically attracted to people of more than one gender or regardless of gender. Historically, definitions of bisexual refer to 'an attraction towards men and women'; however, many bisexual people recognise that there are more than two genders.

Pansexual – A person who is emotionally and/or sexually attracted to people of more than one gender or regardless of gender. Some people use the term pansexual rather than bisexual in order to be more explicitly inclusive of non-binary gender identities.

Queer – An umbrella term sometimes used for diverse sexual minorities that are not heterosexual. It may be used to challenge the idea of labels and categories such as lesbian, gay, bisexual. It is important to note that it is an in-group term, and may be considered offensive to some people.

Bi visibility

There are many misconceptions about bisexuality which can often be challenging. For this reason on 23 September each year we celebrate Bi Visibility Day to improve the visibility of people who are bisexual. We are collecting the voices of young bisexual people. If you would like to contribute your story then please e-mail us info@lgbtyouth.org.uk.

⇨ The above information is reprinted with kind permission from LGBT Youth Scotland. Please visit www.lgbtyouth.org.uk for further information.

Asexuality: when life isn't all about sex

Research suggests 1% of the population (more women than men) are asexual. But the majority of people may view asexuality more negatively than other sexual minorities, and it has been identified as a 'sexual disorder' in the past.

By Anthony Bogaert

Though asexuality isn't something which is often discussed in the media, it is used in entertainment: think Sherlock Holmes eschewing of all things sexual and thus adding to the dramatic portrayal of the character's single-minded pursuit of intellectual truth, or think Sheldon in *Big Bang Theory* brushing up against a sexualised world and thus ramping up the comedic tension in the sit-com.

In the modern, real-world incarnation of the no/low sex spectrum we find asexual people, a group increasingly interested in 'coming out' and staking their claim on the social landscape. A defining feature of asexuality is little or no sexual attraction to other people – in short, no lustful lure for others.

Not surprisingly, many asexual people also exhibit very little sex drive or sexual interest whatsoever (including no masturbation), although some may still have some 'solitary' desire. Thus, some asexual people may still evince some sexual drive but it is not connected to others.

Recent research has suggested that perhaps as many as one per cent of the population – with more women than men – are asexual. Research also suggests that the origins of asexuality, like traditional sexual orientations, are at least partly rooted in early development.

Researchers have also begun to examine a variety of issues related to asexuality, including how some asexual people are content to 'fly under the radar', socially speaking, while others may form a strong asexual identity and 'come out' to others, and how asexual people may be the subject of prejudice and discrimination. In the latter case, recent research suggests that the sexual majority may view asexual people more negatively than other sexual minorities.

Asexual people, particularly if they are comfortable with themselves, have also recently challenged health professionals, including writers of the latest edition of the *Diagnostic and Statistical Manual of Mental Disorders* (or *DSM*), as to what it means to have a sexual disorder. For example, there is now a provision in the recent *DSM* that allows self-identified asexual people to avoid being diagnosed with having a sexual disorder.

As I suggest in my book, *Understanding Asexuality*, there are many reasons why those interested in sex – including sex researchers/educators – should try to understand asexual people and their view of the world. First, studying asexual people provides information on a relatively unstudied group, and knowledge of this minority may help asexual people understand themselves better and ease their negotiation through a complex and foreign sexual world.

Studying asexuality also provides a unique window on sexuality and its mysteries, including its complex relationship to love and romance. For example, although some asexual people do not want romantic relationships – one person on AVEN, the most popular online forum for asexual people, writes succinctly: "Never had a relationship, never want one" – many asexual people desire romantic relationships, even if they eschew sexual ones. Another AVEN participant writes: "I am now in a relationship with a heterosexual person, I don't know how it will work out but I am trying to be positive about it and keep the focus on what we have in common rather than what we don't have in common ..."

Given that asexual people often want a romantic relationship (despite its challenges), they provide a model of how romantic love can be de-coupled from sex, and such a model also holds for sexual people. Indeed, the popularity of movies in the bromance genre – e.g. two (burly) straight men forming a deep bond – demonstrates the usefulness of the romance versus sex model of human attachment.

Examining asexuality also can afford a clear view on how deeply infused sex is in our society – from the pervasiveness of sex in the media to our enduring interest in gossip on the sex lives of others. We also may begin to see more clearly the strange and often mad complexity of sex, with its jealousies, obsessions and distortions of reality. Sex is unquestionably part of the great story of human life – our means of reproduction and a deep source of passion and pleasure for many – but it is also a strange and mad world at times, and one that is better understood if we take a glimpse or two from the outside.

Anthony F. Bogaert, PhD, is a Professor at the Department of Health Sciences, and Department of Psychology, at Brock University, Canada. His latest book is *Understanding Asexuality*.

20 July 2015

⇨ The above information is reprinted with kind permission from *The Independent*. Please visit www.independent.co.uk for further information.

One in two young people say they are not 100% heterosexual

Asked to plot themselves on a 'sexuality scale', 23% of British people choose something other than 100% heterosexual – and the figure rises to 49% among 18–24-year-olds.

By Will Dahlgreen and Anna-Elizabeth Shakespeare

Invented by Alfred Kinsey in the 1940s, the Kinsey scale plots individuals on a range of sexual dispositions from exclusively heterosexual at 0 through to exclusively homosexual at 6. Where the original study had a large number of methods for placing people, YouGov simply asked people to place themselves on the sexuality scale.

Taken as a whole, 72% of the British public place themselves at the completely heterosexual end of the scale, while 4% put themselves at the completely homosexual end and 19% say they are somewhere in between – classed as bisexual in varying degrees by Kinsey. Of the people that do place themselves in this 1–5 area, the majority incline away from homosexuality – 15% are closer to the heterosexual end, 2% directly in the middle and 2% are closer to the homosexual end.

> **"People of all generations now accept the idea that sexual orientation exists along a continuum rather than a binary choice"**

With each generation, people see their sexuality as less fixed in stone. The results for 18–24-year-olds are particularly striking, as 43% place themselves in the non-binary area between 1 and 5 and 52% place themselves at one end or the other. Of these, only 46% say they are completely heterosexual and 6% as completely homosexual.

People of all generations now accept the idea that sexual orientation exists along a continuum rather than a binary choice – overall 60%

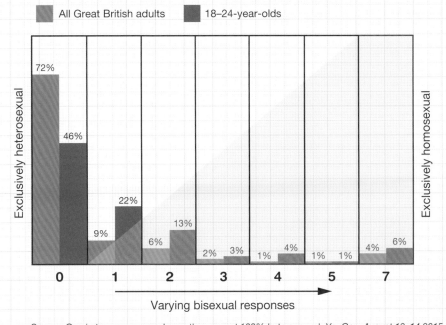

One in two young people not 100% heterosexual

British adults were asked to place themselves on the Kinsey scale, ranging from 0 (completely heterosexual) to 6 (completely homosexual).

- All Great British adults
- 18–24-year-olds

Varying bisexual responses

Source: One in two young people say they are not 100% heterosexual, *YouGov, August 13–14 2015*

of heterosexuals support this idea, and 73% of homosexuals. 28% of heterosexuals believe that "there is no middle ground – you are either heterosexual or you are not".

But what does it mean to be at 1 on the scale, and what is the difference being here or at 2? According to the research, progressing further away from 'completely heterosexual' (0) towards the midpoint (3, or 'completely bisexual') increases the chance that you have had a sexual experience with a member of the same sex. 23% of those at level 1 have had a sexual encounter with a member of the same sex, while 52% of people at level 2 have had such an experience.

Clearly, these figures are not measures of active bisexuality – overall, 89% of the population describes themselves as heterosexual – but putting yourself at level 1 allows for the possibility of

homosexual feelings and experiences. More than anything, it indicates an increasingly open-minded approach to sexuality. In a further set of questions asking if respondents could conceivably be attracted to, have sex with or have a relationship with someone of the same sex (if the right person came along at the right time), level 1s were at least 35% more likely to say they could than level 0s.

16 August 2015

⇨ The above information is reprinted with kind permission from YouGov. Please visit www.yougov.co.uk for further information.

© YouGov 2016

"I'm a bisexual homoromantic": why young Brits are rejecting old labels

Miley Cyrus, Kristen Stewart, Cara Delevingne ... it's not just celebrities who refuse to define themselves as gay or straight. Nearly half of young British adults say they aren't exclusively heterosexual. It can only be a good thing.

By Rebecca Nicholson

When Rugby League's Keegan Hirst came out as gay this week, he said that he had been hiding for a long time. "How could I be gay? I'm from Batley, for goodness sake. No one is gay in Batley." If the 27-year-old Yorkshireman had been a few years younger, he might have found some people in his hometown who are at least sexually fluid. A YouGov poll this week put the number of 18- to 24-year-old Brits who identify as entirely heterosexual at 46%, while just 6% would call themselves exclusively gay. Sexuality now falls between the lines: identity is more pliable, and fluidity more acceptable, than ever before.

The gay-straight binary is collapsing, and it's doing so at speed. The days in which a celebrity's sexual orientation was worthy of a tabloid scandal have long since died out. Though newspapers still report on famous people coming out and their same-sex relationships, the lurid language that once accompanied such stories has been replaced by more of a gossipy, 'did you know?' tone, the sort your mum might take on the phone, when she's telling you about what Julie round the corner has been up to. And the reaction of the celebrities involved has morphed, too, into a refusal to play the naming game. Arena-filling pop star Miley Cyrus posted an Instagram of a news story that described her as "genderqueer" with the caption, "NOTHING can/will define me! Free to be EVERYTHING!!!" Kristen Stewart, who has been followed around by insinuations about the 'gal pal' she is often photographed with for a couple of years, finally spoke about the relationship in an interview with _Nylon_ magazine this month. She said, simply, "Google me, I'm

not hiding", but, like the people surveyed by YouGov, refused to define herself as gay or straight. "I think in three or four years, there are going to be a whole lot more people who don't think it's necessary to figure out if you're gay or straight. It's like, just do your thing."

It's arguable that celebrities such as Stewart are part of the reason for those parameters becoming less essential, at least in the west. It shouldn't fall to famous people to define our social attitudes but, simply, visibility matters: if it is not seen as outrageous or transgressive that the star of _Twilight_ will hold hands with her girlfriend in the street, then that, in a very small way, reinforces the normality of it. If Cara Delevingne tells _Vogue_ that she loves her girlfriend, then that, too, adds to the picture. The more people who are out, the more

normal it becomes; the less alone a confused kid in a small town looking at gossip websites might feel; the less baffled the parent of a teenager who brings home a same-sex date might be. Combine that with the seemingly unstoppable legislative reinforcement of equal rights, too – gay marriage becoming legal in Ireland, in the US – and suddenly, it seems less 'abnormal', less boundary-busting, to fall in love or lust with someone of the same gender.

"I would describe myself as a bisexual homoromantic," says Alice, 23, from Sussex. For the uninitiated, I asked her to explain. "It means I like sex with men and women, but I only fall in love with women. I wouldn't say something wishy-washy like, 'It's all about the person,' because more often it's just that I sometimes like a penis."

She says her attitude towards sex and sexuality is similar among other people in her peer group. "A lot of my friends talk about their sexuality in terms of behaviour these days, rather than in terms of labels. So they'll say, 'I like boys,' or 'I get with girls too,' rather than saying, 'I'm gay, I'm a lesbian, I'm bisexual.'"

She says that even among those who exclusively date people of the same gender, there is a reluctance to claim an identity as proscriptive as 'gay'. "Most young people who are gay don't see it as a defining property of their character, because they don't have to, because society doesn't constantly remind them of their difference." However, she is careful to point out that this is very much the case in the small, liberal part of London where she lives now. "[Not defining] is something I feel entitled to as a person who lives in London, but I didn't feel entitled to it in a small town in the home counties. I've never experienced discrimination about my sexuality, but I'm aware that it's because I 'pass' [as straight]."

In fact, among the young British people I spoke to, geography is vital. Lucy, 25, wonders if the number of people who say they are not straight really tallies with the number of people who are actually acting upon those desires. "Saying you're sexually fluid means you're part of a movement. It means you're seen as forward-thinking," she says, suggesting there is a certain cachet attached to being seen as open that does not come with affirmed heterosexuality. She also believes it is more of a metropolitan story than necessarily representative of Britain as a whole. "If I went back to my home town in the Midlands, we wouldn't sit around talking about 'sexual fluidity'. You're a 'dyke', or you're not. There's only one type of lesbian there."

Many people questioning their sexuality make the traditional migration from a small town to a big city to find like-minded people – to find their tribe, to belong. It is a familiar and understandable story that you hear across generations. But now, within these cities, the pubs

and bars that were once a meeting point for non-straight people are beginning to disappear, swallowed up by the brutal economics of an obscene property market, because they are relatively niche spaces that cannot bring in the footfall of, say, a shiny, straight All Bar One. The VICE channel Broadly recently released a film called *The Last Lesbian Bars*, which asked why women-only spaces across the US were closing. As is the case in London, financial viability was part of it, as was the growth of dating apps, but it struck me from the film and from my own experience that many 'lesbian' nights have become mixed, 'queer' events, where all genders are welcome. At their best, they can feel like a joyful coming together of misfits, of all different types and persuasions.

In fact, the word queer, once the defiant reclamation of a homophobic slur, has become a ubiquitous term. While the young people I spoke to were largely resistant to the word 'bisexual', even if they are sleeping with both men and women, they used 'queer' easily and freely. "Among our callers and our volunteers, more and more people are identifying as 'queer', particularly among younger generations," says Natasha Walker, a trustee of the LGBT+ Helpline, which recently changed its name from the London Lesbian & Gay Switchboard in order to be more inclusive. "In the past, people were fighting for the right to be able to define themselves as lesbian, gay, bisexual, trans* etc. Although this is very much still the case, there is also a definite shift towards an acceptance of people as they are – label or no label."

There is also some appeal in the radical roots of 'queer', particularly as same-sex desire becomes more usual: while mainstream assimilation makes discrimination less likely, it does run the risk of removing the 'outsider' identity of gay life, which many are keen to preserve.

"Essentially, the gays are getting married and it's all become normalised," says John, 32, from

Plymouth. "'Queer' is still a political term. The older I get, the more I use it, because I feel I understand it more than when I was 22, but it's also a cultural shift, absolutely." While the word 'bisexual' is, as John puts it, "a bit woolly", 'queer' encompasses a broad spectrum of desires, and is inclusive of those people who might reject the gender binary, too.

Moving beyond the need to identify as one thing or the other feels utopian in many respects, and it acknowledges that for many people, sexuality is not an either/or decision. But it also relies on an idealised vision of an open-minded and kind society, which is true for the privileged world of, say, celebrities, but is not always the case elsewhere. Casual homophobia has not been erased by semantic optimism. John says a cab recently cancelled his trip after pulling up to the kerb and seeing him kissing his boyfriend. "We ran after him, but he just carried on." Last month, one of John's friends was spat at from a car window as he stood outside a gay pub. These are small, but constant reminders that abuse, discrimination and prejudice are present and pernicious, in small towns and in big cities. So if more young people reject heteronormativity, then that can only be a good thing, whether they act upon it, or not. But there is power in claiming an identity, and it is worth remembering, too, that complacency may be as dangerous as labels.

18 August 2015

⇨ The above information is reprinted with kind permission from *The Guardian*. Please visit www.theguardian.com for further information.

Only 17% of LGBTI Brits know it's National Coming Out Day tomorrow*

By Shanti Rao

October 11 is National Coming Out Day (NCOD) – an annual, internationally observed civil awareness day celebrating individuals who publicly identify as a sexual or gender minority. One of the aims is to raise awareness of the issues surrounding coming out of the closet as an LGBTI (Lesbian Gay Bisexual Transgender Intersex) individual.

However, a OnePoll survey of 1,000 Brits who identify as LGBTI showed that just 17% of them knew that NCOD is tomorrow. While another 15% at least knew NCOD exists, that still leaves a whopping 68% that had never even heard of it.

30% of the people we asked thought NCOD could help raise awareness of the issues surrounding coming out of the closet, while another 56% thought it might if it was better publicised.

27% of people even thought NCOD might help some people build up courage to come out to their friends and family, and similarly, 50% thought it could do if more people knew about it.

Average age to come out

For the men that took our survey, the average age to realise they were LGBTI was 15, and the average age to come out was 19.

On average, women tended to realise slightly later at age 16, but come out a bit sooner at age 18.

Over time, people seem to be realising they're LGBTI at a younger age. For respondents aged 55+, the average age was 18. This age steadily decreased right down to the 18–24-year-old group, who realised at age 13 on average.

The same linear trend emerged when we looked at the average age people came out of the closet, with people aged 55+ doing so at 24, and 18–24-year-olds at age 16.

Homosexual people were more likely to be 'out' than bisexual people

The majority of people that took our survey identified as either homosexual (42%) or bisexual (50%).

42% of people that identified as homosexual feel able to be completely open about their sexuality. 14% said they're open with friends but not family, and just 3% remain firmly in the closet, having not told anyone.

It seems bisexual people are less likely to come out than their homosexual counterparts, with only 29% feeling able to be completely open about their sexuality. Meanwhile, more of them are open with friends but not family (22%), and many more haven't told anyone at all (14%).

Why stay in the closet?

The most common reason given for not being completely out of the closet was the worry that other people might treat them differently once they found out (37%).

The second most common concern was that some friends and/or family members would disapprove (31%).

28% of people that said they're not fully open about their sexuality said this was in part due to the fact they were currently in a heterosexual relationship.

23% said they worry that they may be the victim of bullying if they come out to everyone.

8% said they're still in the closet because their religion states that being LGBTI is wrong.

6% were concerned that it might affect their career prospects.

Why come out?

The most influential factor in deciding to come out of the closet for our panellists was feeling confident in one's own sexuality/ gender (35%), closely followed by feeling it would help with one's personal growth (31%).

25% of people that had come out said they didn't feel able to be themselves while still in the closet, and 17% felt like they were lying to friends and family by pretending to be heterosexual.

Very few people had come out because they felt pressured by a friend or partner to do so (3%), though many would argue this is 3% too many.

How to tell people

63% of people said they came out to their friends and family face-to-face.

The second most popular communication method was by text (28%), and third was on the phone (24%).

30% of 18–24-year-olds said they came out on social media.

How did it go?

50% of people we surveyed that had come out to someone said some of those they told were very accepting.

30% said some of the people they came out to already knew they were LGBTI anyway.

Sadly, 23% found they were rejected by some of the people they opened up to.

Despite some people having negative experiences when coming out, people said that they were more likely to experience positive feelings, such as relief (26%), happiness (19%) or freedom (14%) than negative ones, such as depression (2%), loneliness (4%) and fear (9%) at this time.

Inclusive sex education

Sex education in schools is a controversial topic, but many people are currently campaigning for mandatory LGBTI-inclusive sex education in schools.

55% of people surveyed thought LGBTI-inclusive sex education would help young LGBTI people build up courage to come out to their friends and family.

The potential benefit most people thought it could have was to support young LGBTI students in understanding their own sexuality and gender (59%).

However, only 12% thought they received enough LGBTI-inclusive sex education in school. A considerable 53% weren't taught any at all.

10 October 2014

Please note that this information is from 2014 and that newer statistics may have been published since then. The original blog can be found here: http://www.onepoll.com/only-17-of-lgbti-brits-know-its-national-coming-out-day-tomorrow/

⇨ The above information is reprinted with kind permission from OnePoll. Please visit www.onepoll.com for further information.

Do we still need National Coming Out Day?

This Sunday 11 October [2015] is National Coming Out Day and for many this will be an exciting and celebratory day. But with all the moves forward in equality in the UK, do we still need it?

11 reasons why we still need National Coming Out Day

⇨ Coming out supports equality in all its forms; it sparks conversation, educates and challenges dated and frankly ignorant perceptions.

⇨ A coming out story being shared can be incredibly powerful to someone else who is struggling with their own identity and coming out.

⇨ Students who are lesbian, gay or bi continue to be the most highly bullied demographic with isolation, self-harm and suicide rates far higher than the national average.

⇨ Very few people regret coming out even if the initial experience isn't as positive as they'd hoped.

⇨ Hiding your sexual identity can be far more stressful than being open. Visibility is crucial and powerful; it really can change hearts and minds.

⇨ Despite marriage equality there is still a way to go before the UK achieves full equality for ALL its citizens. Pension laws for those who are lesbian and gay, marriage equality for those who are trans* and equal sex education in schools are just three examples of things that need to be made equal.

⇨ A united day provides a strong community feel online with an increased amount of support, both from organisations and others going through the same thing, being made available.

⇨ Coming out and REAL visibility contribute to the global picture – it gives a voice to those who are silenced and helps those whose right to be themselves are non-existent all over the world.

⇨ Coming out gradually reduces 'casual' homohate and transhate. It empowers those who are scared to simply hold hands in public with their partner.

⇨ Visibility in turn demands representation. You have a voice – use it!

⇨ Don't feel under pressure to come out until you're ready – it might be that the first step is coming out to yourself.

In summary

We get it – who you date, who you love, shouldn't ever be an issue … but we're not quite there yet. Ultimately, we believe that sexuality is on a continuum with people very rarely being 100% anything. We are working towards a culture where we no longer need National Coming Out Day and eventually it won't even be a thing. Whatever you decide to do, there is support available if you need it.

October 2015

⇨ The above information has been reprinted with kind permission from Ditch the Label. Please visit www.ditchthelabel.org for further information.

#LGBTInnovators – British race walker Tom Bosworth

Tom Bosworth is a British race walker who holds three British Records. He is currently ranked 1st overall in the UK for 20 km. He is the British record holder for the 10k race walk, 39:36, set in 2015 along with the 5,000m race walk, 19:16, set in 2014. Tom was selected to carry the Olympic Torch through Potternewton, Leeds. He competed for Great Britain at the World Athletics Championships, is set to feature at the Rio Olympics and is the first athlete on the team to come out as gay.

Tom came out publicly as gay on the Victoria Derbyshire show on BBC last year. Speaking to the show, he said:

"Coming out is no surprise to my friends, family and even team-mates, even Mo Farah, who didn't bat an eyelid when I told him I was gay.

I got to know him and others on the Great Britain endurance team prior to the World Athletics Championships in August after we spent a few weeks on a pre-training camp in Japan.

It was a great chance to talk about it in a relaxed environment and everyone was very supportive of me being the first openly gay athlete on the GB team.

I know there will always be people who have a problem with my sexuality, but one person's opinion doesn't affect me now, as I have support from my parents and partner.

All I want to do is give a positive message that you can succeed in sport whatever your background. Be it gay, straight, black, white, religious or non-religious – there are no barriers.

I can only speak from my experience but I found it a relief to be open with my friends, family and team-mates. It made me feel comfortable not having that cloud over me, the feeling that you are covering things up.

I just hope that the more sportsmen and sportswomen who come out, the more sport will catch up with the real world."

LEAP Sports is spotlighting #LGBTInnovators in sport throughout LGBT History Month this February. We will celebrate a different LGBTI innovator in sport each day. LGBTIsports innovators include athletes, competitors, coaches, managers, community members, founders or co-ordinators of sports groups, someone passionate about their sport.

Got an LGBTI innovator in sport that you would like to shine a light on?

Use your imagination and join the conversation using the hashtag #LGBTInnovators on Twitter @Leapsports and Facebook facebook.com/leapsports

Find out more about LGBT History Month at www.lgbthistory.org.uk.

28 February 2016

⇨ The above information has been reprinted with kind permission from LEAP Sports. Please visit www.leapsports.org for further information.

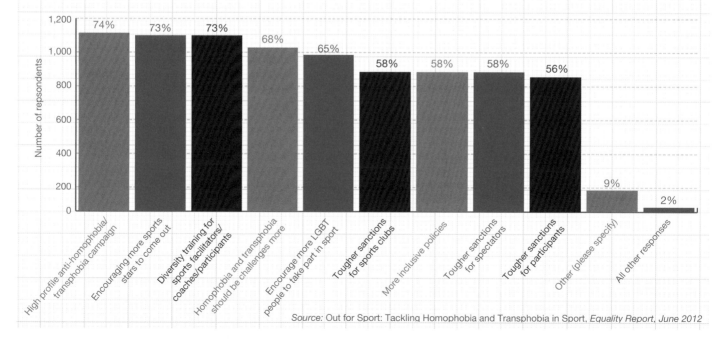

What do you think should be done to tackle homophobia and transphobia in sport? (Tick all that apply)

Source: Out for Sport: Tackling Homophobia and Transphobia in Sport, *Equality Report, June 2012*

How the rainbow became the symbol of gay pride

Where did that rainbow flag come from, and how did it come to symbolise gay pride and rights?

By Ana Swanson

Many people signed on to the Internet on 26 June to find their Twitter and Facebook feeds exploding with rainbows. The Supreme Court's landmark decision to make same-sex marriage a Constitutional right across the country sparked a huge volume of rainbow coloured cartoons, gifs and photos.

Where did that rainbow flag come from, and how did it come to symbolise gay pride and rights? The story is a touching one, involving a drag queen who would come to be known as 'Busty Ross', huge trash bins full of dye, clandestine trips to the laundromat, and the famous gay politician Harvey Milk. Gilbert Baker, an artist and drag queen, first created the Rainbow Flag in 1978.

The rainbow had the added benefit of being a natural and universal symbol that works in any language. The rainbow flag also had some connections with Judy Garland, a favourite figure of the gay community who sang 'Somewhere Over the Rainbow' in *The Wizard of Oz*. *The Advocate* had called Garland "an Elvis for homosexuals".

Before that, the symbol of the gay movement was a pink triangle, which had originally been used by the Nazis in concentration camps to denote gay people and other 'sexual deviants'. The gay movement had reclaimed the pink triangle during the 1970s, but some felt the symbol still had disturbing connotations.

In part because of the pink triangle, bright colours always played a strong role in gay identification, especially purple and lavender. As Forrest Wickman of *Slate* writes, gay people historically used bright colours to signal their sexuality – including bright yellow socks, and the green carnation that Oscar Wilde famously wore on his lapel.

Baker's grandmother owned a woman's clothing store, and he was fascinated with clothing and fabrics from a young age. However, he grew up in a small, conservative town in Kansas and never learned to sew. He left home to join the army, and then headed to San Francisco when he left the army in 1972, just as the city's gay community was flowering.

"Once I was finally liberated from my Kansas background, the first thing I did was get a sewing machine," he told the web site Refinery 29 in an interview. "Because it's 1972 and I have to look like Mick Jagger and David Bowie every single second," he says. "Taffeta jumpsuits."

Because of his sewing talents, Baker started taking over the task of making banners for the protest marches. The rainbow flag first rose to prominence when Harvey Milk, a member of the San Francisco Board of Supervisors and the first openly gay politician in a major US city, asked Baker to make a flag for a march he was organising – just a few months before Milk was assassinated.

Baker recalled making the first rainbow flags with about 30 volunteers in the top-floor attic gallery of the Gay Community Center at 330 Grove Street in San Francisco. They had huge trashcans filled with water and dye, and dyed thousands of yards of cotton, ending up covered in coloured dye. To rinse out the dye, they needed to use a laundromat. They knew they weren't supposed to put dye in public washing machines, lest the next person ended up with pink underwear.

So they waited until late at night to visit, and put Clorox in the machines after they left. The group raised two flags in the United Nations Plaza in downtown San Francisco on 25 June 1978. One was the rainbow flag, while another was an American flag with rainbow stripes instead of red, white and blue.

30 June 2015

⇨ The above information is reprinted with kind permission from *The Independent*. Please visit www.independent.co.uk for further information.

Gender dysphoria

Gender dysphoria is a condition where a person experiences discomfort or distress because there's a mismatch between their biological sex and gender identity. It's sometimes known as gender identity disorder (GID), gender incongruence or transgenderism.

Biological sex is assigned at birth, depending on the appearance of the genitals. Gender identity is the gender that a person 'identifies' with or feels themselves to be.

While biological sex and gender identity are the same for most people, this isn't the case for everyone. For example, some people may have the anatomy of a man, but identify themselves as a woman, while others may not feel they're definitively either male or female.

This mismatch between sex and gender identity can lead to distressing and uncomfortable feelings that are called gender dysphoria. Gender dysphoria is a recognised medical condition, for which treatment is sometimes appropriate. It's not a mental illness.

Some people with gender dysphoria have a strong and persistent desire to live according to their gender identity, rather than their biological sex. These people are sometimes called transsexual or trans people. Some trans people have treatment to make their physical appearance more consistent with their gender identity.

Signs of gender dysphoria

The first signs of gender dysphoria can appear at a very young age. For example, a child may refuse to wear typical boys' or girls' clothes, or dislike taking part in typical boys' or girls' games and activities.

In most cases, this type of behaviour is just a normal part of growing up and will pass in time, but for those with gender dysphoria it continues through childhood and into adulthood.

Adults with gender dysphoria can feel trapped inside a body that doesn't match their gender identity.

They may feel so unhappy about conforming to societal expectations that they live according to their anatomical sex, rather than the gender they feel themselves to be.

They may also have a strong desire to change or get rid of physical signs of their biological sex, such as facial hair or breasts.

Getting help

See your GP if you think you or your child may have gender dysphoria.

If necessary, they can refer you to a specialist Gender Identity Clinic (GIC). Staff at these clinics can carry out a personalised assessment and provide any support you need.

Assessment

A diagnosis of gender dysphoria can usually be made after an in-depth assessment carried out by two or more specialists.

This may require several sessions, carried out a few months apart, and may involve discussions with people you are close to, such as members of your family or your partner.

The assessment will determine whether you have gender dysphoria and what your needs are, which could include:

⇨ whether there's a clear mismatch between your biological sex and gender identity

⇨ whether you have a strong desire to change your physical characteristics as a result of any mismatch

⇨ how you're coping with any difficulties of a possible mismatch

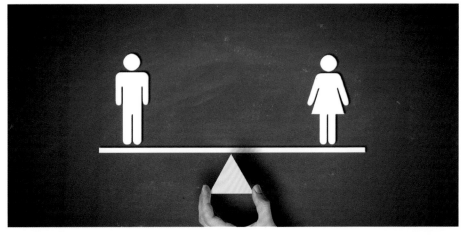

⇨ how your feelings and behaviours have developed over time

⇨ what support you have, such as friends and family.

The assessment may also involve a more general assessment of your physical and psychological health.

Treatment for gender dysphoria

If the results of an assessment suggest that you or your child have gender dysphoria, staff at the GIC will work with you to come up with an individual treatment plan. This will include any psychological support you may need.

Treatment for gender dysphoria aims to help reduce or remove the distressing feelings of a mismatch between biological sex and gender identity.

This can mean different things for different people. For some people, it can mean dressing and living as their preferred gender.

For others, it can mean taking hormones or also having surgery to change their physical appearance.

Many trans people have treatment to change their body permanently, so they're more consistent with their gender identity, and the vast majority are satisfied with the eventual results.

What causes gender dysphoria?

Gender development is complex and there are many possible variations that cause a mismatch between a person's biological sex and their gender identity, making the exact cause of gender dysphoria unclear.

Occasionally, the hormones that trigger the development of biological sex may not work properly on the brain, reproductive organs and genitals, causing differences between them. This may be caused by:

⇨ additional hormones in the mother's system – possibly as a result of taking medication

Gender terminology

Gender dysphoria is a complex condition that can be difficult to understand. Therefore, it helps to distinguish between the meanings of different gender-related terms:

⇨ **gender dysphoria** – discomfort or distress caused by a mismatch between a person's gender identity and their biological sex assigned at birth

⇨ **transsexualism** – the desire to live and be accepted as a member of the opposite sex, usually accompanied by the wish to have treatment to make their physical appearance more consistent with their gender identity

⇨ **transvestism** – where a person occasionally wears clothes typically associated with the opposite gender (cross-dressing) for a variety of reasons

⇨ **genderqueer** – an umbrella term used to describe gender identities other than man and woman – for example, those who are both man and woman, or neither man nor woman, or moving between genders.

Gender dysphoria isn't the same as transvestism or cross-dressing and isn't related to sexual orientation. People with the condition may identify as straight, gay, lesbian, bisexual or asexual, and this may change with treatment.

⇨ the foetus' insensitivity to the hormones, known as androgen insensitivity syndrome (AIS) – when this happens, gender dysphoria may be caused by hormones not working properly in the womb.

Gender dysphoria may also be the result of other rare conditions, such as:

⇨ congenital adrenal hyperplasia (CAH) – where a high level of male hormones are produced in a female foetus. This causes the genitals to become more male in appearance and, in some cases, the baby may be thought to be biologically male when she is born.

⇨ intersex conditions – which cause babies to be born with the genitalia of both sexes (or ambiguous genitalia). Parents are recommended to wait until the child can choose their own gender identity before any surgery is carried out.

How common is gender dysphoria?

It's not known exactly how many people experience gender dysphoria, because many people with the condition never seek help.

A survey of 10,000 people undertaken in 2012 by the Equality and Human Rights Commission found that 1% of the population surveyed was gender variant, to some extent.

While gender dysphoria appears to be rare, the number of people being diagnosed with the condition is increasing, due to growing public awareness.

However, many people with gender dysphoria still face prejudice and misunderstanding.

12 April 2016

⇨ The above information has been reprinted with kind permission from NHS Choices. Please visit www.nhs.uk for further information.

© NHS Choices 2016

My trans daughter

Sharon has a teenage daughter who is transgender. She describes how Nicki was born in a male body, but felt from a very young age that she should have been a girl.

"When my child Nick was about two, I realised that he wasn't playing with toys that I expected a boy to play with. He was interested in dolls and girly dressing-up clothes.

"At that age, it doesn't really matter. You just think they're trying lots of different things, so I never made a fuss about it.

"But when he was four years old, Nick told me that God had made a mistake, and he should have been a girl. I asked my GP what I should do. He told me to wait and see, and that it might just be a phase and go away. But it didn't. It got stronger.

"One day, when Nick was six, we were in the car and he asked me when he could have the operation to cut off his 'willy' and give him a 'fanny'. His older cousin had told him about these things.

"I spoke to a friend who's a psychiatrist. He said I should contact the Tavistock Clinic [now The Tavistock and Portman service for children and young people with gender identity issues].

"He also told me that the medical term is 'gender dysphoria'. When I looked it up online, I found Mermaids, a charity that helps children with gender identity issues and their families.

"I also spoke to my GP again, who referred us to the local mental health unit. The person at the unit had worked at the Tavistock and knew about gender identity issues.

"He was brilliant. It was such a relief to talk to somebody who understood what was going on. I'd blamed myself, but he reassured me that it wasn't my fault. We were then referred to the Tavistock Clinic.

"The team from the Tavistock came to Nick's school and talked to the teachers. They helped the teachers to understand that Nick wasn't being difficult, and that this may or may not be a phase. When a child is this young, you just don't know."

From Nick to Nicki

"Nicki desperately wanted to be female all the time. When she was ten, we feminised her name from Nick to Nicki at home. The following year, Nicki started secondary school as a girl.

"The school was very supportive, but because she moved up to secondary school with her peer group, everybody knew.

"In the first week, she was called a 'tranny' and a 'man-beast'. She was spat on and attacked in the corridors. Within her first six months of being at that school, she took four overdoses.

"We then pulled her out of school, but after a few months she decided to go back. Each year, the bullying and isolation got worse, and Nicki started harming herself. At the beginning of year nine, I transferred her to another secondary school, but unfortunately the kids there found out.

"At that point, I withdrew her from school completely, and the education welfare office found her a place at a Specialist Inclusive Learning Centre, which is a unit for children who can't cope with mainstream schooling for various health reasons."

Going through puberty

"When Nicki started puberty, I wanted her to get the type of treatment that's offered in The Netherlands, where puberty is blocked before major physical changes take place.

"I felt that if she was going to change her mind about being a girl, she would have done so by now. The Tavistock Clinic wouldn't give her hormone blockers."

The Tavistock and Portman follows British guidelines, which at the time suggested not introducing hormone blockers until the latter stages of puberty. Since January 2011, the age at which hormonal treatment may be offered has been lowered from 16 to 12 under a research study being carried out by

the Tavistock and Portman into the effects of hormone blockers earlier in puberty.

"In the end, we went to a doctor in the US," says Sharon. "I found him through the WPATH network [The World Professional Association for Transgender Health]. Nicki was 13 when she started taking hormone blockers. It's put her male puberty on hold and given her time to think.

"If she hadn't been given blockers, she would have suffered the psychological agony of going through male puberty. She told me she would have killed herself. Nowadays, you'd never guess that she was born male.

"If at any point Nicki were to tell me that she wasn't sure that this was the right thing for her, we'd simply stop the injections and male puberty would go ahead. For Nicki, the next step is starting hormones and surgery as soon as she can.

"During the first few years of secondary school, I was constantly in fear for Nicki's life. It was so distressing to watch her go through all of this.

"Now, it's a million times better. She's a typical teenage girl, and it's a blessing. She leaves a mess, she borrows my clothes, my make-up and my perfume. I never thought she'd reach this stage. She still has to face many more hurdles, but she's looking forward to adulthood."

*The names in this article have been changed.

Where to get help

Sharon says the most helpful thing was speaking to other families who've been through the same thing.

The charity Mermaids provides family support for children and teenagers with gender identity issues, and can put you in touch with other parents with similar experiences.

Further information

This story reflects one mother's experience. Because gender identity issues are complex and each case is different, Sharon's story shouldn't be seen as typical.

13 July 2015

⇨ The above information has been reprinted with kind permission from NHS Choices. Please visit www.nhs.uk for further information.

Trans history for LGBT History Month

In preparation for LGBT History Month, we have prepared a short guide to UK trans* history which includes information about UK historical trans* figures and events, and a brief discussion of the difficulties in collating and recording trans* history.

Who are trans* people?

People are trans* if they do not fully identify with the gender they were assigned at birth.

Who were trans* people in the past?

We can see evidence of trans* people in all cultures and periods for which we have sufficient evidence to study gender identity. The terminology used to describe gender identity and presentation has changed significantly between different societies and over time, as has what it means to be a man, a woman, or another gender.

Despite this we can see that there have always been people who did not fully identify with or present as the gender they were assigned at birth. These people would fit our current conceptualisation of what it means to be trans*, although this is a label that they would probably be unfamiliar with. Throughout history, trans* people have been rich and poor, rulers and slaves, artists and farmers. In short, trans* people in the past were a diverse bunch!

Why are trans* people often erased from history?

Although trans* people have been found in all the societies we learn about as children, they are often ignored by schools, textbooks and historians. The reasons for this are complex and multiple. One issue is that trans* people are seen in a negative light in our current culture. This means it is not seen as valuable for us to learn their history.

Few people have studied and written about trans* history, compared to the histories of other groups. This is something of a catch 22, little is written about trans* people, so few people read about them, so few people choose to study them further, so little is written about them. It is vital that we break this cycle and write and learn about trans* people in history.

Another issue is that LGB identities and trans* identities have not been considered as distinct throughout history. The concept of 'sexual inversion' as developed by sexologists in the late 19th and early 20th centuries is an interesting example. Kraft-Ebing referred to female inverts as "the masculine soul, heaving in the female bosom", whilst Havelock Ellis' conceptualisation of the term is closer to our modern understanding of homosexuality. Because of this, people such as the author Radclyffe Hall, who self-defined as an invert, has since been claimed by LGB people as part of lesbian history rather than of trans* history.

Some interesting trans* people and events from modern British history

James Barry (1789–1865)

James was a military surgeon and a pioneer in caesarian sections. He performed what may have been the first ever caesarian in which both mother and child survived. He also worked to improve conditions in military and civilian hospitals in South Africa. He met Florence Nightingale through his work, but the pair did not get on. He began living as a man around 1809, just before beginning his medical training. It seems his colleagues were unaware that he was trans* until after his death.

"Since 1999, on 20 November, trans* people around the world have gathered to remember those killed as a result of transphobia, especially those murdered in hate crimes"

Mary Mudge (1814–1889)

Mary was a very poor woman who lived in a small village in Devon. She never married and worked as a dairymaid. She died in a workhouse at the age of 85, and her trans* status was only discovered after her death. The discovery was then widely reported in newspapers. Her story tells us that trans* people may be found in all walks of life, and that many trans* people live normal lives as members of their chosen gender. People such as these must often go unnoticed by their communities and by future historians.

The Rebecca Riots (1839–1843)

The Rebecca Riots were a series of riots in south- and mid-Wales, protesting unfair taxation imposed by the English Government, and related poverty. Most participants in the riots dressed in women's clothing, and although many donned such clothing only during the riots, there is evidence to suggest that some of the leaders lived as women more widely.

"The body should be made to fit, approximately at any rate, to the mind"

Stella Boulton and Fanny Park (tried in 1871)

Stella and Fanny were put on trial in Victorian London, accused of "conspiring and inciting persons to commit an unnatural offence". This charge shows the contemporary attitude that trans* people were a dangerous threat to the morality of others. The prosecution was unable to prove that any offence had been committed, but Stella's partner, Lord Arthur Clinton, killed himself during the trial. Stella had lived as a girl since early childhood, and Fanny began living as a woman after meeting Stella as a teenager. The pair worked as a theatrical double act.

Drag Ball Riot, Hulme (1880)

A police raid led by detective Jerome Caminada on what has been named by historians as a "drag ball" in Hulme, Manchester, resulted in a riot in 1880. The subsequent trial of the people involved was detailed in newspapers at the time and scandalised the Victorian middle classes.

Michael Dillon/Sramanera Jivaka (1915–1962)

Michael/Sramanera was a doctor, author and the first trans* man in the UK to undergo phalloplasty (penis construction). His 1946 book, *Self: A Study in Endocrinology and Ethics*, made the case that trans* people should be offered medical transition rather than being treated for mental illness. He fled to India after his trans* status was discovered, where he converted to Buddhism, changed his name to Sramanera, and published on Buddhist practices for British children.

"The body should be made to fit, approximately at any rate, to the mind." – Michael Dillion

Roberta Cowell (1918–2011)

Roberta was a racing driver who competed in the 1939 Grand Prix. She became a fighter pilot in the Second World War, and was captured and became a German prisoner of war, suffering solitary confinement and starvation. She was liberated in 1945. Back in England, she suffered from PTSD and sought the help of a psychiatrist. With his support she began transition. She went on to become the first trans* woman in the UK to undergo vaginoplasty (vagina construction). Her surgeries were carried out both by the surgeon who operated on Dillon, and by Dillon himself. She was not allowed to compete in the Grand Prix again following her transition, but she remained an active part of UK motor racing.

Transgender Umbrella

Crossdressing people
comfortable with their physical gender at birth, but will occasionally dress like the opposite gender

Transgender women
male-to-female

Transgender men
female-to-male

Trans non-binary people
Not exclusively one gender:
- identify as both masculine and feminine (androgynous)
- identify between male and female (intergender)
- neutral or don't identify with a gender (agender)

Please note that this is not an exhaustive list and that terminology is evolving all the time and so definitions may change in the future.

Source: Trans umbrella, *The Scottish Transgender Alliance, 2016*

Trans* people banned from marrying (1967)

In the case of Talbot (otherwise Poyntz) Vs. Talbot, Judge Ormerod ruled that trans* people were not permitted to marry under British law.

"Marriage is a relationship which depends on sex, not on gender." – Judge Benjamin Ormerod

Jan Morris (born 1926 – age 88)

Jan is a Welsh historian, author and travel writer. In 1953 she was part of the first British team to successfully climb Mount Everest. She transitioned in the 1960s and chose to undergo surgery abroad, as doing it in the UK would have meant the Government forced her to divorce her wife. They were ultimately forced to divorce anyway, but remained together and entered a civil partnership in 2008. She accepted a CBE in 1999, but says she did it only to be polite and that she remains a Welsh nationalist republican. In 2008 *The Times* named her one of the 15 greatest writers since the war.

The Self Help Association for Transexuals (formed 1980)

SHAFT was formed in 1980, as a mutual aid organisation through which trans* people could collect and share useful information.

Legal rights for trans* people (2002–today)

It was not until 2002 that the UK Government stated that "transexualism is not a mental illness". It was not until 2005 that trans* people in the UK were able to change their legal gender. There still exists complex and time-consuming bureaucracy that trans* people must navigate in order to achieve this. Cuts made to the NHS and other public services under the current government have meant that waiting lists for trans* people to get life-saving medical treatments are now measured in years rather than months.

Transgender Day of Remembrance (1999–today)

Since 1999, on 20 November, trans* people around the world have gathered to remember those killed as a result of transphobia, especially those murdered in hate crimes. Each year, there is at least one memorial in Manchester, which is organised by the local trans* community. It is an important time for the community to remember those they have lost and that the fight for trans* rights is far from over.

Further reading and research

There are few high-quality resources on trans* history. Those that do exist may conflate trans* and LGB people and/or may not respect the preferred pronouns of trans* people.

More research and awareness is urgently needed!

"Marriage is a relationship which depends on sex, not on gender"

A good starting point is to use search engines to research the people and events outlined in this article.

⇨ The above information has been reprinted with kind permission from Action for Trans Health. Please visit www.actionfortranshealth.org.uk for further information.

© Action for Trans Health 2016

Understanding non-binary people

A guide for the media.

What non-binary people say ... "Show us in our spaces, show our art and our activism." "Include us in the media representation of the world. We exist in society so we should exist in places where society is portrayed." "Gender variety of all kinds should be a part of historical, sociological and political programming and dramas." "Show us as 'real' people, with the same dignity and respect as binary gender people. Show that our non-binary identity is just as valid as binary gender identities, we aren't just uncertain, indecisive or attention-seeking."

What are non-binary people?

Non-binary is an umbrella term used to describe people who do not feel male or female. They may feel that they embody elements of both, that they are somewhere in between or that they are something different.

Non-binary people can still have a strong sense of gender. They can find it very distressing to be told that they must identify themselves as male or female. Many identify as transgender.

Being non-binary is different from being intersex. Most non-binary people are born with bodies that look conventionally male or female, but grow up feeling different. Like most people, they usually develop a sense of gender between the ages of three and seven. They may not describe themselves as different until a lot later because they don't have the words with which to do so, and because there are very few visible non-binary role models.

Being non-binary has nothing to do with sexual orientation. Non-binary people have the same range of preferences as other people.

Some non-binary people choose to have surgery or take hormones to alter their bodies and help them feel more comfortable. Others don't feel that this could help them, or are satisfied with their bodies as they are. Some present themselves androgynously while others look conventionally male or female but may still 'come out' by discussing their identities openly. Many try to blend in because they don't want to risk rejection.

As an increasing number of non-binary people choose to live their lives openly and push for official recognition, their stories are becoming visible in the media.

What's in a name?

As the chart shows, non-binary people use a range of different terms to describe themselves. We recommend that, where possible, journalists ask them what they prefer. Most such people are neutral about the term non-binary so this can be used as default.

Pronouns

Most non-binary people do not feel it's appropriate for people to refer to them as he or she. Various new pronouns are used to solve this problem, including xie and xir, zie and zir, and sie and hir. Where using a subject's preferred pronouns is not possible, we recommend using singular they. This usage, where gender is unclear, goes back a long way in English. It has enjoyed the support of literary figures like Jane Austen and today it is used by major organisations like Facebook. It is widely accepted and understood.

Invisibility

Many non-binary people tell us that they feel ignored by the media.

"Allow us to exist in stories and media, don't sensationalise the fact that we are non-binary, give

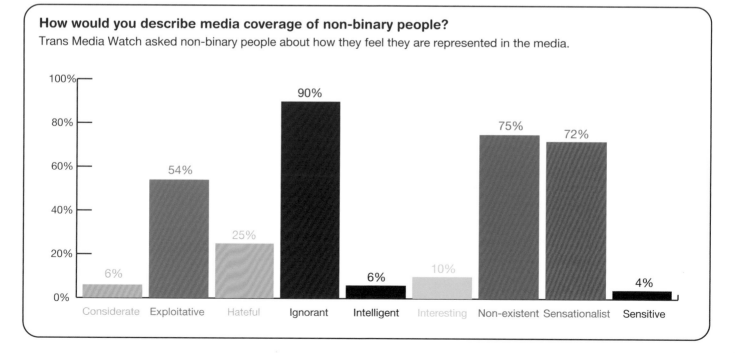

How would you describe media coverage of non-binary people?

Trans Media Watch asked non-binary people about how they feel they are represented in the media.

Considerate	Exploitative	Hateful	Ignorant	Intelligent	Interesting	Non-existent	Sensationalist	Sensitive
6%	54%	25%	90%	6%	10%	75%	72%	4%

us stories outside of our identities and cast non-binary people to play non-binary people. Don't make jokes about not being able to tell someone's gender, or belittle non-binary people's experience," said one of the people we spoke to.

"It would be a massive step forward to see mention of non-binary people in the mainstream media, without their gender being the sole focus of the coverage," said another.

86% of the people we spoke to said it would help them to have visible non-binary role models in the media. This rose to 92% when we asked if it would have been helpful when growing up.

Current coverage

Many non-binary people feel that current media coverage misses the mark, with 80% of those we spoke to describing it as bad or very bad. 74% said that they think this is a subject the media knows nothing about. Several told us that they think it's time big media organisations made the effort to speak to non-binary people directly in order to improve their understanding.

One of the people we spoke to wanted "more thoughtful exploration like BBC Radio 4's *Analysis* episode *Who Says I'm A Woman?*"

"I think non-binary gender is a collection of identities that much of the public would be able to understand, and perhaps even identify with, if positive and accurate dialogue surrounding these identities was present in the media," said another.

Non-binary icons

There are already famous people who cross gender boundaries. We asked non-binary people to name some of their role models:

⇨ Eddie Izzard

⇨ Richard O'Brien

⇨ Brian Molko

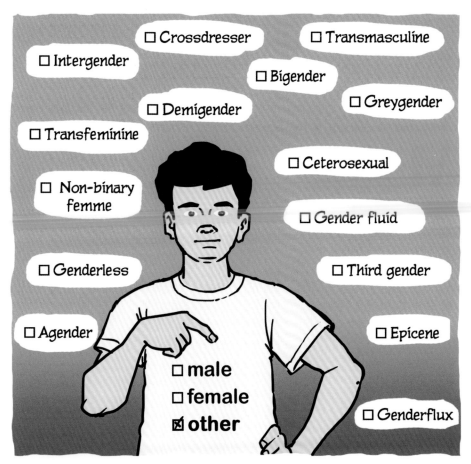

⇨ Pete Burns

⇨ Del LaGrace

⇨ Volcano

⇨ Anthony Hegarty

⇨ Grayson Perry

⇨ Kate Bornstein

⇨ Norrie May

⇨ Welby

⇨ B Scott

⇨ Dennis Rodman

⇨ Morrissey

⇨ CN Lester

⇨ Justin Vivian Bond

⇨ Rae Spoon.

Points to note

⇨ Most non-binary people do not want to do away with gender. They just want their own genders to be respected.

⇨ Having a non-binary identity is something innate within a person. It is not simply a lifestyle choice.

⇨ Non-binary people face an elevated risk of street harassment and assault. This is partly due to poor public understanding.

⇨ Countries like India and Australia legally recognise genders other than male and female.

⇨ British businesses and local councils are increasingly acknowledging multiple gender options.

Find out more

Trans Media Watch is committed to ensuring that all kinds of transgender people, including non-binary people, are represented in the media with accuracy, dignity and respect.

⇨ The above information has been reprinted with kind permission from Trans Media Watch. Please visit www.transmediawatch.org for further information.

© Trans Media Watch 2016

"Doctors still do not acknowledge that I'm intersex"

Maya Posch has fought for almost a decade to be recognised as intersex. She tells Channel 4 News why Germany's change of law is a seminal moment.

Maya Posch has fought for nearly a decade to be recognised in The Netherlands as an intersex person. In an interview with Channel 4 News, she explains the difficulties she has encountered and why she plans to move to Germany.

"Gender is a personal thing. With transgenders we allow people to change sex. So why the hell should we force gender upon an infant? It doesn't make sense," she says.

Each year, one in every 2,000 babies – or 0.05 per cent of the world's population – is born with ambiguous sex organs. Often that means being automatically enrolled into a life that will only be understood years later.

But with choices already made – either by anxious parents or the result of over-eager medical judgments - the consequences can be emotionally devastating.

Now Germany has become the first European country to allow new-born babies to be registered as neither male nor female. They will, in effect, be the 'indeterminate sex', or the third sex.

Small change, big difference

It is a small bureaucratic detail, but intersex people, who are often left to languish with no clear gender-defining characteristic, it is a major step towards change. Society's attitudes to those of intersex can be alienating at best – or psychologically torturous at worse.

In the words of one adult with no clear gender-defining genitalia, whose testimony contributed towards the change of law in Germany, "I am neither a man nor a woman. I will remain the patchwork created by doctors, bruised and scarred".

For Posch, she was lucky to have parents that did not comply with social or medical pressure – and allowed her the freedom to decide for herself.

"I never made a decision. I just stayed between both emotionally and I never chose anything. But medical experts still don't understand that I'm intersex. I have to go to Germany for that."

Moving on

Germany's new law, which follows in the footsteps of Australia, allows parents to select "blank" rather than male and female – allowing the child the option to choose later in life.

Signed in a constitutional court, the law is designed to ease pressure on parents to make quick decisions on sex assignment surgery. It decrees that as long as a person "deeply feels" he or she belongs to a certain sex, theirs is the right to choose a legal identity.

Few can predict what effect the law might have. Yet emotionally its ramifications can already be felt. For Posch, who has fought for nearly a decade to be recognised as a third sex, the significance of the moment cannot be overstated: "This [change of law] is incredible," she says.

"If more people were born and given the third gender choice, it would have made their lives so much better and so much happier."

1 November 2013

⇨ The above information has been reprinted with kind permission from Channel 4 News. Please visit www.channel4.com/news for further information.

Make sex education compulsory and LGBT-inclusive

Labour plans on gay sex education and homophobic bullying need to go further.

By Peter Tatchell, Director of the PTF

Labour has announced its commitment to shake-up sex education and anti-bullying programmes in schools. The party's Shadow Education Secretary, Tristram Hunt, wants to make age-appropriate, gay-inclusive sex and relationship education compulsory and ensure that all teachers are trained to tackle homophobic, biphobic and transphobic bullying.

Set out in the report, *End homophobic bullying together – Supporting LGBT young people and teachers*, this is a good move and much needed (http://bit.ly/1DIxoO1).

Explaining why these proposals will be a 'priority' for the next Labour Government, Mr Hunt said: "No young person should ever feel that their sexuality or gender identity prevents them from fulfilling their potential."

The new policy will apply to all state-funded primary and secondary schools – including faith and academy schools – but not independents. Excluding the independent sector strikes me as a mistake. Surely it's time there were minimum uniform standards in all schools?

The problem of sexual orientation and gender identity bullying is huge and often ignored, as revealed in Cambridge University research

published by the gay lobby group Stonewall.

The School Report (2012), looked at the bullying of lesbian, gay and bisexual (LGB) pupils (trans pupils were regrettably not included). It found that 55% of LGB young people have suffered bullying on account of their sexuality and 99% have heard homophobic language.

Astonishingly, one in three teachers report hearing homophobic remarks from other staff, according to *The Teacher's Report* (Stonewall, 2014). Some LGB teachers are victims of teasing and bullying by pupils because of their sexuality.

Only half of LGB young people say their school has told pupils that homophobic bullying is wrong. This falls to 37% in faith schools. Many teachers do nothing to combat anti-LGB bullying. They tell pupils to be discreet, man-up and be less sensitive. This is not the tough stand that most teaching staff adopt towards racist bullying. Double standards!

LGB pupils who are bullied are at a higher risk of depression, self-harm and suicide. 41 per cent have attempted or considered taking their own life because of bullying and a similar number say bullying has caused them to self-harm. *The School Report* found that one in four young LGB people had actually

tried to commit suicide; rising to nearly half among trans youth.

This week Stonewall estimated there are 215,000 LGB school pupils. As a result of anti-LGB bullying, 52,000 of these pupils will truant from school; 37,000 will change their future education plans; and 70,000 will suffer deterioration in their school work.

For all these reasons, Labour's anti-bullying proposals, which echo similar policies by the Greens and the Lib Dems, are welcome and appreciated. So, too, are its plans to make sex and relationship education (SRE) compulsory and inclusive for lesbian, gay, bisexual and transgender (LGBT) pupils.

Good timing. Last week the National Union of Students (NUS) published a survey of 2,500 university students, which showed that SRE is failing all pupils, both LGBT and heterosexual.

Two-thirds reported that consent and abuse issues were never discussed. More than half said their lessons did not cover emotions and relationships. Under 20% received SRE that mentioned LGBT issues.

SRE standards are so poor that 60% of students said they accessed pornography to find out about sex, with 40% saying it helped their sexual knowledge and understanding.

The mostly low quality of SRE has terrible consequences, including unhappy and abusive relationships, lack of sexual fulfilment, unwanted pregnancies and abortions and unacceptable levels of HIV and other sexually-transmitted infections.

That's why SRE delivery must be improved. This requires a nationwide minimum curriculum content for SRE lessons, specialist training in teaching SRE and action to ensure that all school staff understand LGBT issues and support LGBT pupils.

The one issue the new Labour initiative side-steps is the current right of parents to withdraw their children from SRE if they object to them receiving information about reproduction, safer sex, LGBT issues, contraception and abortion.

Why should parents be able to deny their children the right to information to debunk ignorance and prejudice and to ensure they have happy, healthy sexual and emotional lives?

I thought school was about preparing young people for adult life. Love, sex and relationships are some of the most important aspects of most people's lives. Yet millions of young people grow up sexually and emotionally illiterate. The result? Dysfunctional, miserable relationships and unfulfilled sexual and emotional needs; leading to anxiety, depression and other manifestations of mental ill-health. Plus drug and alcohol abuse.

This is the shocking price we pay for half-baked SRE and the right of parents to pull their kids out of SRE classes.

Labour and other parties should pledge to either scrap the parental opt-out completely or require parents to come to the school and physically take their child out of each SRE lesson. The latter option would preserve the right of parents to withdraw their children but require them to make an effort. In all likelihood, the number of kids being taken out of SRE would plummet which, from a child welfare point of view, would be a damn good thing.

Another notable finding from the NUS survey is that more than a third of students gave their SRE experience a negative rating on equality and diversity.

To prevent prejudice and bullying, schools clearly need to do more to challenge ignorant, intolerant attitudes, so that pupils treat each other fairly and with respect – to create a safer, friendlier and more cohesive education environment – and society.

No one is born bigoted. Some young people become bigoted because of the bad influences of adults and peers. Early, sustained equality and diversity education can help prevent this.

That's why I believe equality and diversity education against all prejudice – including racism,

misogyny and homophobia – should be part of the core national curriculum and required teaching in every school. These dedicated lessons – by specialist trained teachers – should start from the first year of primary level through to the end of secondary education.

The aim would be to promote understanding and acceptance of Britain's many different peoples and communities. Together with a strong affirmation of our common humanity, they should educate young people to accept that the right to be different is a human right, providing this difference doesn't infringe the rights of others.

Does Labour get it? I hope so. Will the other parties get it? I hope so. This shouldn't be a party political issue. We are talking about young people's welfare. They deserve better.

For more information about the Peter Tatchell Foundation's human rights work, to receive our e-mail bulletins or to make a donation: www.PeterTatchellFoundation.org.

5 February 2015

⇨ The above information has been reprinted with kind permission from the Peter Tatchell Foundation. Please visit www. PeterTatchellFoundation.org for further information.

Despite recent victories, plights of many LGBT people remain ignored

An article from **The Conversation.**

By Doug Meyer, Lecturer of Women, Gender & Sexuality, University of Virginia

THE CONVERSATION

To be sure, monumental gains have been made for LGBT rights over the past decade: national marriage rights, widespread media representations and the end of "don't ask, don't tell" in the military.

Yet often glossed over in the coverage of political victories and pop culture accounts, like the recent film *Stonewall*, are those among the LGBT community who have yet to reap the rewards, who remain marginalised, exploited and victimised.

For example, just last week, the National Coalition of Anti-Violence Programs reported that homicides of transgender or gender-nonconforming people are happening at a startling rate. This year, the number has already reached 22 (compared to 12 in 2014 and 13 in 2013).

It's a topic I explore in my recent book *Violence against Queer People: Race, Class, Gender, and the Persistence of Anti-LGBT Discrimination*, which, while acknowledging certain political triumphs, argues that the main beneficiaries of these victories seem to be a certain type of LGBT person: white, gay, middle-class men.

Still suffering

During my research, I interviewed scores of those who still feel threatened – and marginalised – by their sexual identity.

For example, after running away from home, Jayvyn, a 33-year-old black gay man, experienced violence in a group home for several years. There, several of his male housemates referred to him as "the faggot" and would crush up glass,

sprinkling it in his bed while he was sleeping. Jayvyn would awaken with shards of glass stuck to his skin.

Meanwhile, Lela, a 48-year-old black transgender woman, experienced similar violence in a homeless shelter, where she was the only transgender woman living with men. Homeless shelters often segregate residents based on birth sex rather than gender identity, which can expose transgender people to tremendous amounts of violence. Some of the men Lela lived with in the homeless shelter would hold her down while others hit her with hard objects, including socks filled with rocks or marbles.

Who's left out?

If you saw the (widely panned) 2015 film *Stonewall*, you might think that the gay rights movement reflected the struggle of closeted, white, masculine men. This whitewashes the events of not just the Stonewall Riots, but also the larger history of LGBT activism. Many of the participants in 1969's Stonewall Riots were actually transgender women – known as "drag queens" at the time – in addition to people of colour, butch lesbians and feminine gay men.

Rather than paying homage to accounts of the riots, the main character of the film ended up being a white, conventionally attractive, gay man.

But the Stonewall film is merely part of a long history in which marginalised LGBT people have been sidelined. It doesn't exclude only women and LGBT people of colour, but also homeless, transgender and HIV-positive LGBT people.

On the other hand, white and financially well-off gay men have routinely been catered to. The gay rights movement has presented this group as the face of the movement. Most well-known LGBT activists and spokespeople – Dan Savage, Ellen DeGeneres and Dustin Lance Black, to name a few – have been white. And marriage has been their call to arms; LGBT organisations have insisted that this emphasis moves the struggle for LGBT rights forward.

The problem with this approach is that it benefits a relatively small group of LGBT people – the most privileged. For example, many white and financially well-off gay men benefit from gay marriage becoming the law of the land because of the numerous financial rewards of marriage. Yet for LGBT people like Jayvyn and Lela, legalising gay marriage doesn't make much of a difference in their day-to-day lives; it does little to address the threat of violence, nor does it release them from the grip of poverty.

And because of discrimination in the job market, women, transgender people and black and Latino LGBT people are less likely to be wealthy in the first place, and therefore less likely to benefit from these approaches. Meanwhile, issues such as homelessness or police violence have been left off the mainstream gay rights agenda.

A movement with misplaced priorities

When it comes to any political cause, money plays an important role in whose voice is heard.

The problem, however, exists beyond access to financial resources. It has to do with the way issues have been prioritised: those important to privileged LGBT people have been defined as "gay rights" issues; meanwhile, issues affecting marginalised LGBT people have been viewed as concerns that are "not gay rights issues". This dynamic has occurred in large part because the LGBT rights movement has not been strongly linked with activist movements fighting against racism, sexism and social class inequality – which all affect LGBT people.

There's significant evidence that transgender people – especially minority trans women – experience higher rates of violence than lesbians and gay men. For example, the National Coalition of Anti-Violence Programs found that 72% of all anti-LGBT homicide victims in 2013 were transgender women. And of the 22 transgender people murdered this year, 86% were black or Latina transgender women.

Despite these higher rates of violence among transgender people, attention has traditionally fixated on homophobic violence. In hoping to sell the seriousness of homophobic violence to mainstream society, the experiences of white and middle-class gay men such as Matthew Shepard and Tyler Clementi have been prioritised.

The emphasis on the plight of white, male gays comes at a cost: the predominant values of mainstream society – whiteness, the middle-class, maleness – remain idealised and unchallenged.

Meanwhile, other LGBT people – the most marginalised members of our communities – have been left behind.

24 November 2015

⇨ The above information has been reprinted with kind permission from *The Conversation*. Please visit www.theconversation.com for further information.

Legal equality

Since Stonewall was founded in 1989, we've seen amazing legal changes for LGBT equality in the UK. This is good news for everyone, because changing laws to ban discrimination against people makes it clear that homophobia, biphobia and transphobia are not acceptable. It helps to change attitudes so that other people in society welcome LGBT people as equals. There is still a lot of work to be done, particularly for trans people's rights.

Some important legal changes that have affected LGBT people in the UK

2000: Government lifts the ban on lesbians and gay men serving in the Armed Forces.

Before 2000, gay and lesbian people could not serve in the Armed Forces. They would have to keep their sexual orientation secret or they could be fired.

2001: Age of consent for gay/bi men is lowered to 16.

Sex between men was illegal until 1967, when the Sexual Offences Act came into force making it legal for men aged 21 or above. In 1994 that age was lowered to 18 and in 2001 it was lowered again to 16 – making it the same as the age of consent for straight people.

2002: Equal rights are granted to same-sex couples applying for adoption.

Before this neither same-sex couples nor unmarried straight couples could adopt or foster children.

2003: Repeal of Section 28.

Section 28 was a law that made it illegal to talk positively about homosexuality in schools. This meant that teachers were not able to support lesbian, gay and bi students or provide resources about different sexualities. The law came into force in 1988 and a year later in 1989, Stonewall was set up to fight it. In 2003 the legislation was repealed which meant that schools were finally able to support their lesbian, gay and bi students.

2003: A new law comes into force protecting LGBT people from discrimination at work.

Until 2003, employers could discriminate against LGBT people by not hiring them or not promoting them, just because of their sexual orientation or gender identity. LGBT people didn't have much protection from bullying and sometimes they weren't offered the same benefits as other colleagues, or were unfairly affected by rules at work. The Employment Equality Regulations made all these kinds of discrimination illegal.

2004: Civil Partnership Act is passed.

Before this there was no legal recognition of same-sex relationships. Civil partnerships give same-sex couples the same legal rights as married couples. They allow same-sex couples to make the same public declaration of their love and commitment that other couples do when they get married.

2004: Gender Recognition Act is passed.

Fought for by the organisation Press For Change, this Act allowed trans people to change their legal gender. This means that they can get a new birth certificate that reflects who they really are, which helps for future legal processes like marriage.

2005: The Criminal Justice Act gives courts power to give tougher sentences for homophobic crimes.

Until 2005 if a person was attacked for being gay or because the attacker thought they were gay then it was treated like any other crime. The Criminal Justice Act changed that so that these were classed as 'hate crimes' and were treated more seriously.

2007: It becomes illegal to discriminate against people because of their sexual orientation or gender identity when providing them with goods or services.

Before 2007 any service provider could discriminate against an LGBT person who bought something from them or used their service. For example, a hotel owner could refuse to allow a gay couple to stay in their hotel, or a local authority could refuse to house a same-sex couple together. Today, people can't be refused goods or services because they're lesbian, gay, bi or trans.

2008: The Criminal Justice and Immigration Act makes "incitement to homophobic hatred" a crime.

Before 2008 there was no law against behaviour or materials that stirred up hatred towards gay people. There were many publications and websites that said hateful things about gay people and encouraged damaging and unhelpful myths about them. All of these things are now illegal.

2009: A new law gives better legal recognition to same-sex parents.

Until this law came into force, same-sex couples were treated differently by the law to other couples when it came to having a baby through fertility treatment. This law made it easier for same-sex couples to be recognised as the legal parents of their child.

2010: The Equality Act is passed.

There used to be lots of different laws protecting LGBT people from discrimination. The Equality Act 2010 made things simpler by bringing all the protections for LGBT people into one law. It also made sure LGBT people were entitled to the same legal protections given to other groups of people who might face discrimination. In addition to this, public service providers like schools and hospitals have to show how their service is accessible to and supportive of LGBT people.

2013: The Marriage (Same-Sex Couples) Act is passed.

Although same-sex couples could enter into civil partnerships before 2013, they weren't allowed to get married. The Marriage Act 2013 gave same-sex couples the opportunity to get married just like any other couple. Same-sex couples already in a civil partnership can now convert this to a marriage if they want to.

For further information please call Stonewall's Information Service on 08000 502020, tweet to @StonewallUKInfo or e-mail info@stonewall.org.uk.

⇨ The above information has been reprinted with kind permission from Stonewall Youth. Please visit www.youngstonewall.org.uk for further information.

© Stonewall 2016

Challenging homophobic language

What is homophobic language?

'poof', 'lezzer', 'gay boy', 'batty boy', 'you're so gay'

Homophobic language means terms of abuse that are often used towards lesbian, gay and bisexual people, or those thought to be LGB.

However, homophobic language is also often used to refer to something or someone as inferior. Phrases such as 'you're such a lezzer!' or 'those trainers are gay!', for example, may be used to insult someone or something, but without referring to actual or perceived sexual orientation.

This language is often dismissed as "harmless banter" and not thought to be particularly hurtful, especially where the intent is not to comment on someone's actual or perceived sexual orientation.

However, regardless of the lack of any deliberate intent, these terms liken being gay to something that's bad, wrong or inferior.

Homophobic language tends to be used without thinking and is often ignored by teachers and school staff because either they feel it is difficult to know how to respond or they believe the language is used without any homophobic intent.

Why is it a problem?

In secondary schools

⇨ 98 per cent of gay pupils hear 'that's so gay' or 'you're so gay' at school

⇨ 97 per cent of gay pupils hear derogatory phrases such as 'dyke' or 'poof' used in school

"I get called names all the time at school, especially 'poof' or 'faggot'. My stuff is always being ripped up or drawn on or stolen." Alan, 13, secondary school (Scotland)

⇨ 95 per cent of secondary school teachers report hearing the phrases 'you're so gay' or 'that's so gay' in their schools

⇨ eight in ten secondary school teachers report hearing other insulting homophobic remarks such as 'poof', 'dyke', 'queer' and 'faggot'

"Use of phrases like 'that's so gay' have become commonplace." Megan, administrative support, secondary school (East Midlands)

In primary schools

⇨ three quarters of primary school teachers report hearing the phrases 'you're so gay' or 'that's so gay' in their schools

⇨ two in five primary school teachers report hearing other insulting homophobic remarks such as 'poof', 'dyke', 'queer' and 'faggot'

"At primary level, to call another child gay is currently a term of abuse." Jill, teacher, primary school (Yorkshire and the Humber)

"I teach primary age children who use the terms 'poof', 'queer', etc. when name-calling." Emily, teacher, primary school (East Midlands)

Even if pupils are not in each instance deliberately commenting on any actual or perceived sexual orientation, they are inundated daily with messages that equate being lesbian, gay or bisexual with something negative. Name-calling is the most common form of homophobic bullying.

A school culture that permits casual use of homophobic language makes it all the easier for pupils to suffer homophobic name-calling and bullying.

Who is subjected to homophobic language?

"The majority of anti-gay remarks are directed at students who are (probably) not gay but the remarks are intended as insults to insinuate that they are gay." Anna, librarian, secondary school (West Midlands)

Teachers and school staff say that the pupils most affected by homophobic language are, in descending order:

⇨ pupils who are thought to be lesbian, gay or bisexual

⇨ boys for behaving/acting 'like girls'

⇨ pupils who are openly lesbian, gay or bisexual

⇨ boys who don't play sports

⇨ boys who are academic

⇨ girls for behaving/acting 'like boys'

⇨ girls who do play sports

⇨ pupils whose parents/carers are gay

⇨ pupils who have gay friends or family.

"I think that the term 'you're so gay' is very commonly used to express dislike or scorn. Usually when challenged about these comments, pupils are either embarrassed or defiant, expressing their views that to be gay is 'gross'." Kim, teacher, secondary school (Yorkshire and the Humber)

It is not exclusively gay young people who experience homophobic name-calling or harassment. Homophobic bullying can affect any young person at any time during their education, including primary and secondary schools, as well as Further Education and sixth-form colleges.

The impact of homophobic language

When homophobic behaviour and language go unchallenged, a culture of homophobia is created and can impact on young people's sense of belonging, self-esteem and attainment at school.

"If a teacher doesn't intervene when pupils use anti-gay language, it could go further the next time (more specific anti-gay bullying, for example)." Jessica, teacher, independent secondary school (Scotland)

⇨ nine in ten secondary school teachers and more than two in five primary school teachers say pupils, regardless of their sexual orientation, experience name-calling and homophobic bullying at school

⇨ almost two thirds of lesbian, gay and bisexual pupils experience homophobic bullying

⇨ young people who have been homophobically bullied are more likely to leave school at 16

⇨ seven out of ten gay pupils who experience homophobic bullying state that it has had an impact on their school work

⇨ half of those who have experienced homophobic bullying have skipped school at some point because of it

"At one point it really got to me and I couldn't take it anymore. So I had to change my phone, and be taken from some of my lessons because it got so bad." Jay, 18, FE college (North East)

Intervening when young people use homophobic language, including the use of the word gay to mean inferior, creates a school culture where homophobia and homophobic bullying are not tolerated.

Responding to homophobic language

Gay pupils are three times more likely to feel that their school is accepting and tolerant if it responds to homophobic incidents, including homophobic language.

⇨ half of teachers fail to respond to homophobic language when they hear it

⇨ only seven per cent of teachers are reported to respond every time they hear homophobic language

"Where I have heard the phrase 'she's a lezzie' or something similar it has been said at some distance from me and did not lead me to believe that anyone was being hurt

or upset by what was being said. It is a rare occurrence." Juliette, teacher, faith independent secondary school (East of England)

"I reported it and teachers said they couldn't do anything, and when they saw verbal bullying they'd just stand and watch then walk away." Ian, 17, secondary school (East Midlands)

Schools have a duty to safeguard the well-being of all young people in their care. Failure to respond to homophobic language can have an impact on pupils' confidence and self-esteem, as well as their attainment at school.

In the same way that they challenge racist language, school staff should feel confident to respond to homophobic language whenever it happens.

Stonewall's top ten recommendations for tackling homophobic language

1. Teachers and school staff must challenge homophobic language every time they hear it

Language such as 'lezzer' and 'gay boy', as well as 'gay' as a term of disapproval of someone or something, must be challenged in each and every instance to send the message that homophobic language is unacceptable.

2. Make sure that pupils understand why homophobic language is offensive

Pupils will be less likely to use homophobic language when, like racist language, they understand the implications of what they say.

3. Include homophobic language in anti-bullying policies and procedures

Teachers are able to challenge homophobic language more effectively when it is included in school policies.

4. Involve senior managers if homophobic language persists

The involvement of headteachers and senior management proactively as well as in response to the use

of homophobic language sends a strong anti-homophobia message to the school.

5. Involve parents if pupils persist

It is important for parents to help ensure that all school policies are upheld. All pupils deserve to feel safe at school. Whatever their attitudes towards lesbian, gay and bisexual people, parents can play an essential role in ensuring young people are protected from homophobic bullying.

6. Incorporate lesbian, gay and bisexual people into the curriculum

Including themes around LGB people in lessons makes young people more aware of the LGB community and reduces homophobic behaviour.

7. Address homophobia and LGB equality in your lessons

Teaching about homophobia and equality will discourage homophobic language and bullying in schools.

8. Use assemblies to address problems or promote positive messages about gay people

Assemblies can be an ideal opportunity to tackle issues regarding homophobic language or bullying particular to your school or to incorporate positive messages about gay people, for example during LGBT History Month.

9. Use posters and public displays

Poster and public display campaigns can be used to communicate positive messages regarding lesbian, gay and bisexual people and to tackle homophobic language and bullying.

10. Involve pupils

Pupils want their schools to be safe and welcoming places. Ask pupils how they feel about homophobic language and bullying in their school and involve them in initiatives to tackle the problem.

⇨ The above information has been reprinted with kind permission from Stonewall. Please visit www.stonewall.org.uk for further information.

© Stonewall 2016

Mental health issues amongst LGBT youth are not inevitable

By Kate Marston, Projects Coordinator, EACH

A major survey of lesbian, gay, bisexual, transgender and questioning young people in the UK has found that just under half have experienced mental health issues. However we should not forget that LGBT young people demonstrate extraordinary resilience on a daily basis in the face of hostility and silence.

Led by the charity Metro, the Youth Chances project conducted an online survey of 7,000 young people aged 16 to 25 about their experiences of education, employment, health services as well as relationships and sexuality. The survey found a worrying rate of mental health problems amongst LGBT youth with:

⇨ 52% of respondents reporting having engaged in self-harm

⇨ 42% seeking medical help for anxiety or depression

⇨ 44% reporting thoughts of suicide.

The survey results indicate that LGBT young people in the UK have been "badly served" to date by a range of services. Education was a particular concern as respondents highlighted a lack of intervention in bullying incidents and minimal education on same-sex relationships and sexual health. EACH's own experience of supporting targets of homophobia and transphobia demonstrates that too often support and guidance has to be sought out by young people rather than offered and such silence can reinforce feelings of isolation, insecurity and hostility on a daily basis.

The lack of support in schools around LGBT issues is in no small part due to the legacy of Section 28 of the Local Government Act 1988 which prohibited local authorities from "promoting the teaching in any maintained school of the acceptability of homosexuality". Despite Section 28 being repealed in 2003, many respondents to the Youth Chances

survey, who would have attended school from 2004 onwards, reported a sense of unwillingness amongst schools to address LGBT equality and challenge discrimination.

65% of Youth Chances respondents stated that their teachers never spoke out against homophobia or transphobia and 83% indicated that there were no posters in school reflecting diversity of sexual orientations or gender identities.

Celebrating LGBT equality and challenging discrimination is often not a priority for schools despite the Ofsted Inspections Framework and Equality Act 2010 requiring proactive work be done around these topics. There is clearly more work for the Department for Education to do to ensure schools can confidently support LGBT young people. Personal social health education should become a statutory subject and Sex and Relationship Education must be updated to more accurately reflect same-sex relationships, as well as be in line with current equalities legislation.

For too long appropriate measures have not been put in place to support young people and too many have suffered in silence: finding themselves the target of someone else's prejudice and being emotionally and physically affected. Surveys such as Youth Chances are testament to the devastating impact this can have on a young person's life. Yet we must not forget that LGBT young people are more than these damning statistics. Many live, and continue to live, happy, loving and fulfilled lives. Achieving this however requires a supportive network not a 'sink or swim' attitude.

Regardless of sexual orientation or gender identity we can all find ourselves overwhelmed by the

challenges that life throws at us. Knowing how to bounce back is a crucial life skill for health and happiness. This ability to bounce back is not something some people have and others do not, but something we learn. Many gay and transgender young people will already be putting effective coping strategies in place to deal with these challenges. However, too often LGBT young people lack support and feel they cannot cope. Our schools need to invest more in these young people.

EACH is committed to supporting schools to build upon good practice and establish positive and inclusive learning environments for all. If you would like to enquire about our training and consultancy please visit our training pages. Alternatively, if you, or a young person you know, has been the target of homophobic or transphobic bullying EACH's Actionline is the place to click or call – in confidence.

11 January 2014

⇨ The above information has been reprinted with kind permission from Educational Action Challenging Homophobia (EACH). Please visit www.each.education for further information.

How many LGBT people are parents?

The official government estimate is that in the UK in 2013 there were around 20,000 dependent children living in same-sex couple families ("Common Law Marriage" and Cohabitation *report, p.5*).

Current statistics

How many children have been adopted by LGBT people in Britain?

As of 11 December 2015, there had been 1,825 adoptions by LGBT people in Great Britain since reporting began. However, these official statistics exclude:

⇨ the sexual orientation or gender identity of single adopters

⇨ bisexual people not in a same-sex relationship

⇨ trans people – unless they are part of a same-sex couple.

Opposite is a summary of the total number of adoptions by country to adopters either in same-sex relationships, a civil partnership or a same-sex marriage.

Total number: 1,825

Sources: English data is from gov.uk, Scottish data is from the National Records of Scotland website and Welsh data is from the Stats Wales website.

Fostering in Britain

9,070 fostering families are needed across the UK in 2016. The need is for 7,600 foster families in England, 800 in Scotland, 500 in Wales and 170 in Northern Ireland.

Source: The Fostering Network.

There is no monitoring of the number of LGBT foster carers in England, Scotland or Wales.

Adoptions by same-sex couples in England, Scotland, Wales – 2014/15

Between 1 April 2014 and 31 March 2015:

⇨ In England there were 450 children adopted by same-sex couples. There were 160 adoptions by same-sex couples, not in a civil partnership or marriage. 260 adoptions were to same-sex couples in a civil partnership. There were ten adoptions to female same-sex married couples and 20 to male same-sex married couples. Adoptions by same-sex couples accounted for 8.4 per cent of all adoptions in 2014/15, an increase from 6.7 per cent of all adoptions in 2013/14.

⇨ In Wales there were 30 adoptions by same-sex couples. 15 of these were by male same-sex couples in a civil partnership or marriage. Five were by male same-sex couples not in a civil partnership or marriage. There were ten adoptions by female same-sex couples in this period. The 30 adoptions account for 7.8 per cent of all adoptions in this period in Wales. In the 2013/14 period, adoptions by same-sex couples accounted for 7.2 per cent of all adoptions in Wales. For more information visit the Stats Wales website.

⇨ In Scotland there were 17 adoptions by same-sex couples. Ten of these were to female same-sex couples. Seven were to male same-sex couples. The 17 adoptions account for 3.74 per cent of all adoptions in Scotland in this period. In the 2013/14 period, adoptions by same-sex couples accounted for 2.9 per cent of all adoptions in Scotland. For more information visit the National Records of Scotland website.

How many LGBT people have been approved to adopt?

In England between 1 April 2013 and 31 March 2014, 935 people who identify as lesbian, gay or bisexual were approved to adopt. Of these:

⇨ 365 identify as lesbian

Year	England	Scotland	Wales
2014/2015	450	17	30
2013/2014	340	14	25
2012/2013	230	8	20
2011/2012	160	1	5
2010/2011	100	5	5
2009/2010	120	0	5
2008/2009	120	0	0
2007/2008	80	0	0
2006/2007	90	0	0
Country totals:	1,690	45	90

⇨ 560 identify as gay

⇨ Ten identify as bisexual.

Gender identity isn't covered in these statistics. For a more detailed breakdown visit the gov.uk website.

How many LGBT people in my area were approved to adopt last year? How many have started placements with a child/children?

NB: For data protection and disclosure purposes, Ofsted round figures up to the nearest five (one to four have all been rounded up to five). Totals have been rounded up to five to allow maximum use of agency level data with the minimum risk of disclosure. This means that some totals do not match exactly with secondary breakdowns; however, the impact on percentages has been minimal. The purpose of the rounding is to ensure non-disclosure of sensitive data whilst maintaining its usefulness.

Need figures for your local town? Visit the gov.uk website and download the Adoption annual dataset 2013-14: local authority adoption agencies and read tab C3.

Detailed breakdown:

Percentage of orders made for placement with same-sex couple

Region	Number of people who identify as lesbian who were approved to adopt in 2013–14 / number where adoption placements had started	Number of people who identify as gay approved to adopt in 2013/14 / number where adoption placements had started	Number of people who identify as bisexual approved to adopt in 2013/14
North East	25 / 20	20 / 15	0 / 0
North West	80 / 30	90 / 25	0 / 0
Yorkshire and the Humber	30 / 15	30 / 20	0 / 0
East Midlands	25 / 20	40 / 30	0 / 0
West Midlands	35 / 20	40 / 20	0 / 0
East of England	25 / 15	30 / 10	5 / 5
London	35 / 15	110 / 45	5 / 5
South East	50 / 35	65 / 30	5 / 5
South West	20 / 15	45 / 25	5 / 5

adopters. 'One' means one-child-adopted. If one couple takes three children they would count as three adoptions.

Please note that the following groups are not included in these statistics:

⇨ lesbian, gay, bisexual or trans single people.

⇨ bisexual people who are not in a same-sex relationship

⇨ trans people unless they are part of a same-sex couple

England only:

2014 – 340 children adopted by same-sex couples out of 5,050 adoptions (6.7%)

⇨ 2013 – 230 out of 4,010 (5.7%)

⇨ 2012 – 160 out of 3,470 (4.6%)

⇨ 2011 – 100 out of 3,100 (3.2%)

⇨ 2010 – 120 out of 3,180 (3.8%)

⇨ 2009 – 120 out of 3,270 (3.7%)

⇨ 2008 – 80 out of 3,170 (2.5%)

⇨ 2007 – 90 out of 3,290 (2.7%)

TOTAL – 1,240 children adopted by same-sex couples in England since 2007.

Wales only:

⇨ 2014 – 20 children adopted by same-sex couples out of 345 adoptions (5.8%)

⇨ 2013 – 15 out of 330 (4.5%)

⇨ 2012 – 5 out of 245 (2%)

⇨ 2011 – 0 out of 255 (0%)

⇨ 2010 – 5 out of 230 (2.2%)

⇨ 2009 and before – none.

TOTAL for Wales – 45 children adopted by same-sex couples since 2010.

Scotland only:

⇨ 2013 – 14 children adopted by same-sex couples out of 489 adoptions (2.9%)

⇨ 2012 – 8 out of 495 (1.6%)

⇨ 2011 – 1 out of 496 (0.2%)

⇨ 2010 – 5 out of 466 (1.1%)

⇨ 2009 and before – none.

TOTAL for Scotland – 28 children adopted by same-sex couples since 2010.

Northern Ireland

None yet but hopefully we'll have some good news soon. The official legal position in Northern Ireland is that couples can adopt and the term 'couple' extends to unmarried couples (including same sex couples) and those in a civil partnership.

December 2015

⇨ The above information has been reprinted with kind permission from New Family Social. Please visit www.newfamilysocial.org.uk for further information.

Transgender girl, six, wins right to use girls' toilets

By Kelly Rose Bradford

A six-year-old transgender child has won a civil rights case which will allow her to use the girls' toilets at her Colorado school. Coy Mathis's family had taken her and her four siblings out of the Eagleside Elementary school in Fountain while the case was ongoing.

The Colorado Civil Rights Division ruled on Sunday that the Fountain-Fort Carson School District had caused an unnecessarily hostile situation for Coy by not allowing her to use the girls' lavatories. Steven Chavez, the division director, said that the school had created "an environment rife with harassment".

Coy, who was born male but has identified as female since the age of four, had suddenly been banned from entering the girls' facilities at the school, despite having been recognised as a girl throughout her time at the school.

Her parents, Kathryn and Jeremy Mathis, filed a complaint through the Transgender Legal Defense and Education Fund in February after they received a call from the school telling them that when Coy returned from the winter break, she would have to use the boys' toilets.

"She would use the girls' restrooms, she would be called a girl, she would go in the girls' lines," Kathryn Mathis told chat show host Katie Couric at the time.

"It came out that Coy was no longer going to be able to use the girls' restroom and they were going to require her to be using the boys' room, the staff bathroom or the bathroom for the sick children. We didn't know why, we had no idea where this was coming from.

"We got a call one evening, it was the principal and he said he wanted to set up a meeting with us to discuss options for Coy's future use of the restroom," added her husband, Jeremy.

The school's lawyer, W. Kelly Dude, told reporters back in February that the decision had been made in order to protect all the school's students and "took into account not only Coy but other students in the building, their parents, and the future impact a boy with male genitals using a girls' bathroom would have as Coy grew older".

The Mail reports that the family's action was the first to challenge transgender people's access to bathrooms under Colorado's anti-discrimination laws.

Coy's delighted mum said that the family were pleased and relieved that she will now be treated the same as other girls in her school.

"Schools should not discriminate against their students, and we are thrilled that Coy can return to school and put this behind her," Kathryn said. "All we ever wanted was for Coy's school to treat her the same as other little girls. We are extremely happy that she now will be treated equally."

14 August 2014

⇨ The above information has been reprinted with kind permission from The Huffington Post UK. Please visit www.huffingtonpost.co.uk for further information.

When you've gotta go, you've gotta go. But while a trip to the bathroom is a rather straight-forward experience for most people, it can be a difficult and even dangerous experience for members of the trans community.

According to a report published by the Transgender Law Center in the US, transgender people have been refused access to the appropriate facilities at their place of work or school, while others have been attacked in public bathrooms.

The number of gender-neutral bathrooms has grown in recent years, but this has not been without controversy. In North Carolina, USA, a new law dictates where transgender people can use the bathroom: the law requires that people use bathrooms according to their biological sex (the sex they were born with), rather than the gender they identify with. In defence of this new law, it is argued that this is really about equality and safety for everyone; however, others feel that this is a direct violation of human rights.

Source: 'Everyone's talking about this gender-neutral bathroom sign – here's why' by Brogan Driscoll, The Huffington Post UK, 13 May 2015.

Film has a lot to learn from TV when it comes to LGBT representation

***An article from* The Conversation.**

By Martin Zeller-Jacques, Lecturer in Film and Media, Queen Margaret University

THE CONVERSATION

The recent publication of a study measuring the quantity and quality of LGBT representation in mainstream Hollywood cinema has left the industry smarting. Gay and Lesbian Alliance Against Defamation's (GLAAD) research found that out of 102 major studio releases in 2013, only 17 contained identifiable LGBT characters.

But what really got the press going was the fact that only seven of these passed the Russo test, patterned after the well-known Bechdel test for the representation of women. The Russo test looks for characters who are identifiably LGBT, who are not solely defined in terms of their sexuality/gender and whose removal from a film would significantly affect its plot.

But where Hollywood is failing, television continues to incorporate more LGBT characters than ever. A sister report on the state of American television showed that nearly all of the major American television networks increased the proportion of their LGBT representation, as well as the diversity of those representations. Cable channels, too, featured more hours of LGBT-inclusive programming than they did the previous year. ABC Family ranked top, with 50% of its programming featuring LGBT characters.

Some of this gap may be accounted for by difficulties in comparing the two forms of media. The film survey only examines those films which were released under the main label of the seven highest grossing film studios, excluding any reckoning of the output of 'independent' studio divisions, such as Fox Searchlight or Sony Pictures Classics. But these are the very companies through which major studios typically channel the kind of niche projects in which we might expect to find a higher proportion of LGBT representation.

Meanwhile, the television report gives substantial space to the output of both network television channels (which we might loosely equate with the major studios of the film industry) and to cable channels. And some of these cater to the same kind of niche audiences which the methodology of the film research ignores. GLAAD also note that reality and lifestyle television often showcase members of the LGBT community, thereby increasing television's representativity in a way that the cinema cannot match.

Lagging behind

So it's possible that the gap between film and TV has been exaggerated. But a larger truth is still underscored by this: it is undeniable that mainstream movies continue to do very little to advance the representation of LGBT characters. While gay men are getting married and adopting children on major network sitcoms and dramas, they aren't even making it on screen in major movie releases.

The sole exception is in comedies, where gay characters figure almost 50% of the time. The worst offenders were animated or family-oriented films, none of which met GLAAD's criteria for inclusiveness. But they don't appear to have counted *Frozen*'s Oaken, who is suggested by the film to be part of a gay couple, with four kids.

The fact that even GLAAD haven't recognised Oaken as a gay representation points to a problem with the way Hollywood incorporates gay characters into mainstream cinema. To pass the Russo test, a character must be clearly marked as gay, but not in the film only for their gayness. If the film fails to mark the character clearly enough for the audience, as in the case of Oaken, then it can be argued not to include a gay representation at all. But mark the character too clearly, and it can tread close to stereotyping.

But in many genres where sexuality is only implicitly an issue, it's hard to imagine exactly what a minor character capable of passing the Russo test might look like. With only a few minutes of screen time, how does a character announce his/her sexuality and make an impact on the plot which is unrelated to that sexuality? It's different on television, where even minor gay characters tend to be more fully rounded. Over dozens of episodes they tend to develop different facets of their character, and rarely remain token gay characters, even if they begin that way.

So this is the real area where cinema can take a cue from television. Feature films simply don't have time to develop the deep relationships and complex characters which grow, almost despite themselves, on long-running network shows. For LGBT representation in the cinema to come close to that on television, gay characters need to be at the centre of the action. The mainstream success of gay-themed television comedies and dramas has demonstrated that audiences are willing and able to accept gay characters in major roles, experiencing the same hardships and rewards as straight characters.

Hollywood studios should learn from this. Instead of relying on tokenism and including minor gay characters as sidekicks or comic relief, if they really want to strive for better representation they need to include gay characters in central roles. How much would it really change a generic action movie if the hero rescued his boyfriend, rather than his girlfriend, in the final reel? After all, it could still end with a kiss.

7 August 2014

⇨ The above information has been reprinted with kind permission from *The Conversation*. Please visit www.theconversation.com for further information.

The Vito Russo Test

Taking inspiration from the Bechdel Test, which examines the way female characters are portrayed and situated within a narrative, GLAAD developed its own set of criteria to analyse how LGBT characters are included within a film. The Vito Russo Test takes its name from celebrated film historian and GLAAD co-founder Vito Russo, whose book *The Celluloid Closet* remains a foundational analysis of LGBT portrayals in Hollywood film. These criteria can help guide filmmakers to create more multidimensional characters, while also providing a barometer for representation on a wide scale. This test represents a standard GLAAD would like to see a greater number of mainstream Hollywood films reach in the future.

To pass the Vito Russo Test, the following must be true:

⇨ The film contains a character that is identifiably lesbian, gay, bisexual and/or transgender.

⇨ That character must not be solely or predominantly defined by their sexual orientation or gender identity, i.e. they are made up of the same sort of unique character traits commonly used to differentiate straight characters from one another.

⇨ The LGBT character must be tied into the plot in such a way that their removal would have a significant effect. Meaning they are not there to simply provide colourful commentary, paint urban authenticity, or

(perhaps most commonly) set up a punchline. The character should 'matter'.

Less than half (seven) of the 17 major studio films GLAAD counted LGBT characters in managed to pass the Vito Russo Test this year, compared to six out of 14 inclusive films released in 2012. Clearly there is a lot of room for improvement in Hollywood film. With this annual report, GLAAD will continue to track the industry's progress.

Additional recommendations

Seeing more films pass the Vito Russo Test would be a great start, but as several of the films GLAAD tracked in 2013 prove, passing that test in no way guarantees a film won't also be problematic or offensive in its portrayal of LGBT people. Here are some additional recommendations GLAAD has for Hollywood film to both improve depictions of LGBT people and stop repeating the same defamatory mistakes.

Genre films like comic-book adaptations and action franchises are the areas where Hollywood film studios seem to commit the majority of their capital and promotional resources nowadays, but LGBT characters are still rarely seen in them. Especially given their global popularity, these films must become more diverse and inclusive.

None of the LGBT characters that GLAAD counted in 2013 releases are considered 'lead' characters, and there were only a few that had substantial supporting roles. In fact, many of these appearances were no more than a few seconds long, or just enough time to get to a punchline. As is still often said of Hollywood's treatment of other marginalised groups, there need to be more substantial LGBT roles in film.

Diversity in LGBT images continues to be an issue in nearly all forms of media, and film is no different.

Not only should there be a greater number of substantial LGBT roles, those characters should be more gender-balanced, racially diverse and from many backgrounds.

There were no transgender characters in the 2012 releases GLAAD tracked, but the two found in the 2013 releases were hardly an improvement. One was a trans woman very briefly depicted in a jail cell, while the other was an outright defamatory depiction included purely to give the audience something to laugh at. Media representation of transgender people has long remained decades behind that of gay and lesbian people, and images like these continue to marginalise the community. However, recent media attention around trans issues and people like actress Laverne Cox demonstrates that times are changing, and Hollywood should as well.

Anti-gay slurs are less common in film now than they were 20 years ago, but they are by no means extinct, and some are still used by characters the audience is meant to be rooting for. Perhaps even more prevalent are anti-transgender slurs, which in 2013 were used by main characters in films like *Anchor Man 2* and *Identity Thief* for no reason other than to make a joke. With few exceptions, these words should be left on the cutting room floor.

The results: 20th Century Fox, Lionsgate, Paramount Pictures, Sony Columbia Pictures, Universal Pictures, Walt Disney Studios, Warner Brothers.

2015

⇨ The above information has been reprinted with kind permission from the Gay and Lesbian Alliance Against Defamation (GLAAD). Please visit www.glaad.org for further information.

No more Mr Nice Gay: how TV representation changed from *Will & Grace* to *Empire*

Portraying gay men as witty and well-dressed makes them feel inadequate in real life, claims a new study. Really? There's more to modern gay characters than the sexless sidekick.

By Joe Stone

Threats to gay men's self-esteem come in many guises, from Grindr chats that end abruptly after sending a shirtless pic, to the 16% of Britons who think gay sex should be made illegal (thanks guys), to the five remaining countries that believe we should be put to death. Until now, I hadn't factored in that we may all be silently agonising over whether or not we compare favourably to Will Truman from TV relic *Will & Grace* – but according to new research, that is precisely what has been knocking our confidence.

Psychologists from Anglia Ruskin University in Cambridge have found that the positive portrayal of gay men on TV "can be damaging". Apparently, gay men may have been left depressed by movies and TV shows that promote an assumption that we all must be well-dressed, emotionally available and whip-smart. The project leader, Dr Daragh McDermott, argues: "On the face of it, stereotypes associated with gay men, such as being fashionable or witty, appear positive. However, by their very nature, these stereotypes pigeonhole what it means to be gay and lead to unrealistic expectations of how gay men are expected to behave. Gay men who don't fit the common stereotype are often marginalised for not living up to these expectations, which can have an impact on their mental health."

If gay men are being portrayed with unrealistic positivity – which I don't believe – perhaps that would go some way to counteract the negative stereotypes that have existed in film and TV for years.

A study published in 2014 by the US gay rights campaigning organisation GLAAD found that the majority of LGBT characters featured in major studio releases are still offensive or defamatory portrayals (funny that, from an industry that bankrolled *Lesbian Vampire Killers*).

In his recent documentary, *Do I Sound Gay?*, film-maker David Thorpe explored how Disney villains, from Captain Hook to Shere Khan, often have stereotypically 'gay' voices, meaning that generations of kids have been raised to associate being gay with being evil, if kind of fabulous.

Setting aside purely negative portrayals, the results of this latest study lead me to question whether the researchers can possibly have been watching the same programmes as I have – programmes where modern gay characters are often just as complex, damaged and infuriating as their straight counterparts. Apparently not. In fact, judging from the examples cited in the findings, their televisions have been operating on a time delay of ten to 20 years. Alongside *Will & Grace*, they refer to characters from *Sex and the City* and *My Best Friend's Wedding*. This last one was released in 1997, which, as a pop-cultural benchmark, was the same year the Spice Girls' debut album was nominated for the Mercury prize.

While I agree that these examples promote an unhelpful stereotype of gay men as funny, sexless sidekicks, I'm unconvinced that these are qualities most gay men aspire to (most gay men I meet just want to be Russell Tovey, but that's another story). If these shows have had a negative impact, it's not because they have left swathes of gay men tremoring with insecurity that they'll never measure up to Stanford Blatch.

Yes, series such as *Will & Grace* and *Sex and the City* reinforce a two-dimensional notion of what it is to be gay – basically, you're kinda into Liza Minnelli – but things have moved on significantly since then. Take *Looking*, the HBO show about a group of gay friends living in San Francisco. Among their number are Eddie, a HIV-positive outreach worker for LGBT youth, and Dom, a struggling waiter in an open relationship with an older man. All in all, a slightly more complex take on modern gay life than Jack McFarland and his Cher doll.

Fox's hip-hop melodrama *Empire* has been roundly celebrated for confronting the musical genre's history of homophobia head-on. Jussie Smollett stars as Jamal, the black sheep middle child of a record executive, who is pushed out because of his sexuality. Jarring flashbacks to his abusive childhood sit alongside more – dare I say it? amusing – flashes of pernicious prejudice, such as his formidable mother Cookie's insistence on referring to his boyfriend as 'Dora'. Despite this, it's clear that she loves him, which feels like a rounded take on a knotty subject.

On British screens, Russell T. Davies's *Cucumber* was similarly nuanced, exploring the life of a middle-aged gay man in all its messy, complicated glory. The protagonist, Henry, was a grumpy, selfish narcissist, entirely disillusioned with his own life. Most of the characters were gay, but were they in any way cute or aspirational? God, no. Or, at least, not from where I was sitting.

Although the new study relies on dated characterisations, the researchers and I can agree on the need for more multifaceted gay characters – not least to quiet the vocal minority. Perhaps as more gay characters reach our screens, both aspirational and abominable, less will hinge on the few that we do see. Because no TV show can be all things to all gay people – and shouldn't be expected to try.

9 February 2016

⇨ The above information is reprinted with kind permission from *The Guardian*. Please visit www.theguardian.com for further information.

Legal certificate or not, trans people deserve better from the prison system

An article from **The Conversation.**

THE CONVERSATION

By Samantha Pegg, Senior Lecturer, Criminal Law, Nottingham Trent University

The death of transgender woman Vikki Thompson, 21, who was serving her sentence at the all-male Armley Prison in Leeds has drawn attention once again to the treatment of transgender persons by the criminal justice system.

Since the UK Gender Recognition Act 2004 came into force, transgender people have been able to have their acquired gender recognised by going through a detailed legal process which, if satisfied, allows a new birth certificate to be issued. For legal purposes the applicant is then recognised in their new gender. While this was a valuable step toward recognising gender autonomy it seems to have created a hierarchy for trans people, one that permeates our legal and criminal justice system.

As Thompson had no 'gender recognition certificate' she was placed in prison estate that reflected her birth gender. This is in line with the National Offender Management Service guidance that requires prisoners to be placed according to their gender as recognised by the law. There are clearly problems in terms of prison estate – housing those transitioning from male to female in female prisons have in some cases been deemed to raise issues of safety for other inmates.

There is some discretion in this policy, where transgender people are "sufficiently advanced in the gender reassignment process" they may be placed "in the estate of their acquired gender". This was the case for Tara Hudson, the transgender woman initially held in an all-male prison who complained of sexual harassment. Hudson was moved to a female facility after significant public attention prompted the Prison Service to recognise that, as she had lived as a woman all her adult life and had undergone gender reconstruction surgery, she was – in all but law – female.

It is this legal recognition of gender that is the sticking point. The death of Thompson will undoubtedly prompt a rethink of the current rules governing the placement of prisoners – and indeed an investigation is underway. But until there is clearer guidance and rights for trans people, there may be more tragic stories like Thompson's.

Self-identification

The convictions of Gayle Newland and Justine McNally for sexual offences that involved deceiving others about their gender, show how complicated it can be if someone self-identifies as a trans person but is not legally transitioned.

Both were recognised as suffering from gender confusion and, although both had sought psychiatric help for issues including anxiety and self-harm, neither was undergoing medical or legal transition. The fact they had then misrepresented their gender was considered to be something which had prevented their victims making a fully informed decision about consent. That these young women had lied was central to the convictions here – that the defendants may have self-identified as male at the time of the offences was given little credence.

The law here seems to be fixated on binary gender roles with little tolerance for gender variance. However, whether their actions would have been adjudged criminal if Newland and McNally had legally transitioned is also still unclear. It is certainly relevant to prosecutions for sexual offences and the Crown Prosecution Service has advised that, when an offence involves a transgender suspect, "prosecutors will need to know the suspect's position in relation to the Gender Recognition Act 2004 (GRA)".

While it is unsurprising that criminal law has struggled to deal sensitively with gender confusion, the rules governing prison placements are slightly clearer – although they still focus on whether the prisoner has undergone legal recognition.

Holding 'proof'

If we consider possession of a gender recognition certificate definitive proof of gender we need to open up access to those services that allow people to address this, specifically gender identity clinics. There are a limited number of these clinics and UKTrans, an organisation working to campaign and provide advice for trans and non-binary people, report at anything from six weeks to 3.5 years, with most clinics reporting a waiting time of more than a year. It is clear that those suffering gender confusion will currently have a long wait to access services.

What of those who haven't accessed these services, should we treat them in their acquired gender regardless of their position vis-a-vis the law? This will be a question for the transgender equality inquiry by the women and equalities select committee that recently concluded. Tasked with looking at our treatment of trans people, the inquiry will be considering issues affecting trans people in the criminal justice system and access to services.

Addressing these issues is becoming increasingly important. In a society that supports the rights of individuals to live unmolested in their chosen gender role we need to think very carefully about how to treat those who are not legally recognised in their acquired gender.

20 November 2015

⇨ The above information has been reprinted with kind permission from *The Conversation*. Please visit www.theconversation.com for further information.

Government has "no plans" to ban gay conversion therapy

By Ned Simons

The Government has "no current plans" to ban gay conversion therapy, a Conservative health minister said today after the practice was attacked by both Tory and Labour MPs.

Before the General Election, David Cameron said that the therapies were "profoundly wrong" and pledged to "protect people from harm" under a Conservative Government.

Recent research carried out by Britain's leading LGBT charity, Stonewall, revealed that one in ten healthcare workers had witnessed colleagues express their belief in the so-called treatment.

The statistic rises to 22% in London health and social care environments, and has been hailed "incredibly harmful and dangerous" by Ruth Hunt, Stonewall's chief executive.

The Royal College of Psychiatrists have said previously that conversion therapy creates "a setting in which prejudice and discrimination flourish".

Tory MP Mike Freer led a debate on the practice in Parliament on Tuesday and called for it to be banned. "Being gay is not a disease, it is not an illness and it is not something that I or any other gay man or woman can be cured of. To suggest otherwise is not only demeaning, but morally and medically wrong," he said.

"Imagine the outcry if Parliament were to give tacit approval to curing heterosexual men and women of their heterosexuality. There would be uproar. Allowing conversion therapy to try to turn our straight colleagues gay would not last a day, yet we allow therapists to peddle the myth that they can 'cure' people of being gay."

Labour MP Wes Streeting said "the suggestion that there could be a gay cure that makes all LGBT people, and young people in particular, feel that they are different and somehow alien".

He added: "That is what causes them mental ill health."

However Health Minister Jane Ellison said while the Government did not believe that being lesbian, gay or bisexual "is an illness to be treated or cured" – a ban was not currently being considered.

"I fully understand the concerns about so-called gay conversion therapy, but the Government have no current plans to ban or restrict it via legislation, or to introduce statutory regulation for psychotherapists," she said.

Ellison said she acknowledged there was a "continued challenge to the Government to go further" in preventing gay conversion therapy.

Former Tory minister Nick Herbert said there needed to be "a stronger statement of guidance from the Government" that it was wrong.

4 November 2015

⇨ The above information has been reprinted with kind permission from The Huffington Post UK. Please visit www.huffingtonpost.co.uk for further information.

Pardon all convicted gay men, not just Alan Turing

"It's great that Alan Turing was granted a pardon but what about all the other victims of homophobic legislation? An estimated 50,000–100,000 men were convicted under Britain's anti-gay laws during the 20th century. All these men deserve a pardon, like the one that was granted to Alan Turing. His pardon is much deserved but he should not be singled out for special treatment. Unfairly, no such pardon has been extended to the tens of thousands of other gay victims – not even to other high-profile victims such as Lord Montague and Sir John Gielgud," said Peter Tatchell, Director of the human rights organisation, the Peter Tatchell Foundation.

Mr Tatchell is one of the signatories to an Open Letter to the Government, alongside Stephen Fry, Benedict Cumberbatch and Alan Turing's niece, Rachel Barnes. The letter seeks to secure a pardon for every man convicted under Britain's now repealed homophobic legislation. It was published as a full page advertisement in Saturday's *Guardian* newspaper.

The Peter Tatchell Foundation is supporting a petition for a universal pardon.

"A pardon should be granted to all men convicted of consenting adult same-sex relations. This includes those found guilty of Turing's offence of 'gross indecency' and also men found guilty of other anti-gay laws, such as 'buggery', 'procuring' and 'soliciting and importuning' homosexual acts. These bigoted laws were repealed only in 2003," noted Mr Tatchell.

"There were around 49,000 convictions for so-called 'gross indecency' but many more men were convicted under other homophobic laws. Up to 100,000 may have been convicted in total. We don't know the exact number because criminal statistics on homosexual offences are imprecise.

"Shockingly, the criminalisation of men for same-sex acts continued for half a century after Turing's conviction.

"The 1967 Sexual Offences Act was a very partial, limited decriminalisation. It applied to England and Wales only; not being extended to Scotland until 1980 and to Northern Ireland until 1982.

"After 1967, all the ancient anti-gay laws remained on the statute books under the heading: 'Unnatural Offences'. They were merely not enforced in certain narrow circumstances. But most aspects of gay male life remained criminal. In the four years after 1967, convictions for consensual gay offences rose by almost 400%.

"In 1989, over 2,000 men were convicted under the same law as Alan Turing; which was nearly as many as in the repressive 1950–55 era when Turing was prosecuted.

"The 'gross indecency' law of 1885 prohibited any form of sexual contact between men, even mere touching and kissing. It was used to convict Alan Turing in 1952 and to jail Oscar Wilde in 1895.

"The offence of 'gross indecency' was repealed only in 2003. Likewise, the criminalisation of 'buggery' (anal sex) – enacted in 1533 during the reign of King Henry VIII – was repealed only 12 years ago.

"Since the Sexual Offences Act 2003, for the first time in over 500 years, the UK has a criminal code that does not discriminate on the grounds of sexual orientation.

"Homophobia isn't over yet. In 2013, to create a database of 'serious sex offenders', police turned up unannounced on people's doorsteps to demand DNA samples from men who, like Turing, were convicted of consenting adult same-sex relationships decades ago. They were lumped together with rapists and paedophiles. It took a campaign, spearheaded by the Peter Tatchell Foundation and Galop, to get the police DNA trawl dropped," said Mr Tatchell.

2 February 2015

⇨ The above information has been reprinted with kind permission from the Peter Tatchell Foundation. Please visit www. PeterTatchellFoundation.org for further information.

Key facts

⇨ At least 76 countries have laws in effect that criminalise private, consensual same-sex relationships, and in at least five countries conviction may carry the death penalty. (page 2)

⇨ Research suggests 1% of the population (more women than men) are asexual. (page 6)

⇨ One in two young people say they are not 100% heterosexual. (page 7)

⇨ 72% of the British public place themselves at the completely heterosexual end of the Kinsey scale, while 4% put themselves at the completely homosexual end and 19% say they are somewhere in between – classed as bisexual in varying degrees. (page 7)

⇨ For the men that took our survey, the average age to realise they were LGBTI was 15, and the average age to come out was 19. On average, women tended to realise slightly later at age 16, but come out a bit sooner at age 18. (page 10)

⇨ The most common reason given for not being completely out of the closet was the worry that other people might treat them differently once they found out (37%). (page 10)

⇨ 55% of people surveyed thought LGBTI-inclusive sex education would help young LGBTI people build up courage to come out to their friends and family. However, only 12% thought they received enough LGBTI-inclusive sex education in school. A considerable 53% weren't taught any at all. (page 11)

⇨ Many non-binary people feel that current media coverage misses the mark, with 80% of those Trans Media Watch spoke to describing it as bad or very bad. 74% said that they think this is a subject the media knows nothing about. (page 21)

⇨ Each year, one in every 2,000 babies – or 0.05 per cent of the world's population – is born with ambiguous sex organs. (page 22)

⇨ Stonewall estimated there are 215,000 LGB school pupils. As a result of anti-LGB bullying, 52,000 of these pupils will truant from school; 37,000 will change their future education plans; and 70,000 will suffer deterioration in their school work. (page 23)

⇨ The National Coalition of Anti-Violence Programs reported that on homicides of transgender or gender-nonconforming people. In the UK by November 2015, the number had already reached 22 (compared to 12 in 2014 and 13 in 2013). (page 25)

⇨ 98 per cent of gay pupils hear 'that's so gay' or 'you're so gay' at school. 97 per cent of gay pupils hear derogatory phrases such as 'dyke' or 'poof' used in school. (page 28)

⇨ Only seven per cent of teachers are reported to respond every time they hear homophobic language. (page 29)

⇨ As of 11 December 2015, there had been 1,825 adoptions by LGBT people in Great Britain since reporting began. (page 31)

⇨ GLAAD research found that out of 102 major studio releases in 2013, only 17 contained identifiable LGBT characters. (page 34).

⇨ An estimated 50,000–100,000 men were convicted under Britain's anti-gay laws during the 20th century. (page 39)

Glossary

Disclaimer: Please note that this is not an exhaustive list and that terminology is evolving all the time and so definitions may change in the future.

Asexual/asexuality

A person who has no (or very low) sexual feelings, desires or attraction to anyone. However, just because someone isn't sexually attracted to anyone does not mean they cannot be romantically attracted to others (e.g. seeking a relationship for love and companionship that isn't sexual).

Bisexual

Someone who defines themselves as bisexual or 'bi' is attracted to people of either sex. While a bisexual person may be equally attracted to men and women, this does not have to be the case: they may feel a stronger attraction to one sex than the other, or feel attraction to different sexes at different points in their lives.

Civil partnership

The Civil Partnership Act 2004 (CPA) allowed LGB people the right to form legal partnerships for the first time, giving them rights comparable to those of married couples. A civil partnership is a new legal relationship, exclusively for same-sex couples, distinct from marriage.

Coming out

'Coming out' happens when an LGB person feels ready to tell their friends and family about their sexual orientation. As heterosexuality is the most common sexual orientation, those close to them will probably have assumed they were straight. Coming out is a big step for most gay people, especially if they fear a negative reaction from some people. It is quite common for gay people to not be fully 'out', and only let certain people know about their sexuality.

Gender dysphoria

Sometimes known as a gender identity disorder or transgenderism, gender dysphoria is a where a person feels strongly that there is a mismatch between their biological sex (their body) and gender identity (their emotional and psychological identity) – a person may experience distress or discomfort as they feel they are "trapped" inside a body that doesn't match their gender identity. Gender dysphoria is recognised medical condition, for which treatment is sometimes appropriate (for some people this means dressing and living as their preferred gender, for others it can mean taking hormones or having surgery to change their physical appearance). It's not a mental illness.

Gender identity

The gender that a person 'identifies' with or feels themselves to be. This is not always the same as the sex assigned to them at birth (see Gender dysphoria or Transgender).

Heterosexual

Someone who is attracted exclusively to people of the opposite sex to themselves. Heterosexuality is the most common sexual orientation. It is often referred to as 'straight', although some people feel that this is not the best term to use and has the potential to be offensive – it may imply negative connotations for other sexual orientations which may then be seen as 'crooked' in contrast and therefore negative.

Homophobia/transphobia

Homophobia is the irrational fear or hatred of homosexuality (an aversion towards lesbian, gay or bisexual people). Transphobia is the irrational fear or hatred of transpeople. This fear can lead to behaviour that discriminates against LGBT people and consequently advantages heterosexuals. Such discrimination is illegal under the Equality Act (Sexual Orientation) Regulations 2007.

Homosexual

Someone who defines themselves as homosexual is attracted exclusively to people of the same sex as themselves. People of this sexual orientation may prefer to call themselves gay, or a lesbian if they are female. While some gay people may use other words such as 'queer' or 'dyke' to describe themselves, these are not considered universally acceptable and other gay people may find them offensive.

Intersex

An intersex person is born with sexual anatomy, reproductive organs and/or chromosome patterns that do not fit the typical definition of male or female. This may be apparent at birth or become so later in life. An intersex person may identify as male or female or as neither.

Kinsey scale

A 'sexuality scale' invented in the 1940s by Alfred Kinsey. The Kinsey scale plots individuals on a range of sexual dispositions from exclusively heterosexual at 0 through to exclusively homosexual at 6 (and in between these numbers represents a range of bisexuality).

LGBT/LGBTI/LGBTQ+

LGBT stands for 'lesbian, gay, bisexual and transgender', and is often used as a shorthand way of referring to sexual orientations other than heterosexual. As language and terminology evolve, there are now several other variations of this acronym: the I refers to intersex; Q stands for queer; and the + represents asexual, pansexual, transsexual, intersex, questioning and intergender.

Non-binary

If someone is non-binary this means that they do not exclusively identify as one gender. This can be a person who: identifies as both masculine and feminine (androgynous); identifies between male and female (intergender); or as neutral or don't identify with a gender (agender).

Pansexual/pansexuality

A person who is emotionally and/or sexually attracted to people of more than one gender or regardless of gender. Some people use the term pansexual rather than bisexual in order to be more explicitly inclusive of non-binary gender identities.

Rainbow Flag

Gilbert Baker, an artist and drag queen, first created the Rainbow Flag in 1978. With the benefit of being a natural and universal symbol that works in any language, the rainbow became a symbol of gay pride. Historically, bright colours always played a strong role in gay identification, such as Oscar Wilde pinning a green carnation to his lapel. Before that, the symbol of the gay movement was a pink triangle, which had originally been used by the Nazis in concentration camps to denote gay people and other 'sexual deviants'. The gay movement had reclaimed the pink triangle during the 1970s, but some felt the symbol still had disturbing connotations.

Russo test (also known as the Vito Russo Test)

Patterned after the well-known Bechdel test for the representation of women, the Russo test is used to measure LGBT representation in media such as film or television. The Russo test looks for characters who are identifiably LGBT, who are not solely defined in terms of their sexuality/gender and whose removal from a film would significantly affect its plot.

Sexual orientation/sexuality

Sexual orientation refers to a person's physical, romantic and/or emotional attraction towards other people. Sexual orientation is usually defined either as heterosexual or 'straight' (attraction to the opposite sex); homosexual or 'gay'/'lesbian' (attraction to the same sex); or bisexual (attraction to both sexes).

Transgender (sometimes shortened to trans or trans*)

A transgender person is someone who identifies as the opposite gender than that into which they were born, and who has chosen to live their life in that gender. They may or may not have gone through gender reassignment surgery. Someone's gender identity is separate from their sexual orientation: however, issues concerning transgender people and their rights tend to be discussed in relation to debates about sexuality, as they often suffer similar kinds of discrimination to LGB people. These issues do also cross over into debates concerning equal gender rights, however.

Assignments

Brainstorming

⇨ In small groups, discuss what you know about sexuality and gender. Consider the following points:

- What is sexuality?

- What is gender identity?

- What is the difference between gender and sex?

- What is the Kinsey scale?

Research

⇨ What stereotypes exist surrounding gay men, lesbian women and transgender people? Can you think of any films or television programmes you watch, or books you have read, which perpetrate these stereotypes? Can you think of any which challenge them? Make some notes and discuss with a partner.

⇨ Choose an LGBT person from history, or an influential figure from today, and write a detailed report about them. Read #LGBTInnovators – British race walker Tom Bosworth on page 12 and Trans history for LGBT History Month on page 17 for inspiration.

⇨ Find out everything you can about being intersex and create a short presentation for your class.

Design

⇨ Read The Vito Russo Test on page 35. Now, think of a recent storyline in your favourite TV drama or soap which focused on the experiences of an LGBT character. Do you think the storyline was done well? Use this as inspiration to create a storyboard for your own plotline, covering an LGBT-relevant issue such as coming out, first relationships or unrequited crushes.

⇨ In a recent campaign against homophobic bullying in schools, the charity Stonewall adopted the slogan 'Some people are gay. Get over it'. This was used on t-shirts, posters and other campaign materials. Create your own slogan to help tackle homophobic bullying and incorporate it into a poster which could be displayed in schools.

⇨ Create a pamphlet for teens who are questioning their sexual orientation. You might want to explore different LGBT terms, as well as including links and phone numbers to resources they might find helpful.

⇨ Design a poster explaining about the trans umbrella. How has it changed over time?

⇨ Choose one of the articles in this book and create an illustration to highlight the key themes/message of your chosen article.

Oral

⇨ Coming out to parents can be a challenging time for gay and lesbian young people. In pairs, role play a scenario in which a young person tells their parents about their sexual orientation for the first time. Imagine the feelings of both parties during your conversation.

⇨ Imagine you have a friend who comes to you and says they have found a therapist who can help 'cure' homosexuality. How would you endeavour to help your friend understand that there is nothing wrong with their sexual orientation, and put her on her guard against therapists claiming to offer these 'cures'? Role play this scenario with a partner.

⇨ "I've got nothing against gay people personally, but I don't think it's appropriate for same-sex couples to adopt small children who may be influenced by their lifestyle choices." Do you agree with this opinion? Hold a debate in pairs, with one person taking a supporting view and the other an opposing one.

⇨ "Age-appropriate, LGBT-inclusive sex and relationship education should be compulsory in schools." Discuss this statement in groups and feedback to the class.

Reading/writing

⇨ Read My trans daughter on page 16. Write an account of these events from Nicki's viewpoint.

⇨ Write a one-paragraph definition of asexuality.

⇨ The number of children who are born to, or fostered/adopted by, same-sex couples is growing. However, most children's books and stories feature traditional opposite-sex family structures. Create a short illustrated children's book for pre-school children which includes a same-sex parent family as part of the story (the story does not need to be about this issue, however: the aim is to make children aware that some children live within same-sex family models).

⇨ Read the article Understanding non-binary people (page 20) and write a summary for your school newspaper.

Acknowledgements

The publisher is grateful for permission to reproduce the material in this book. While every care has been taken to trace and acknowledge copyright, the publisher tenders its apology for any accidental infringement or where copyright has proved untraceable. The publisher would be pleased to come to a suitable arrangement in any such case with the rightful owner.

Images

All images courtesy of iStock, except page 3: Michal Zacharzewski, page 24 © SXC and page 39 © MorgueFile.

Vector icon on page 19 made by Vectors Market from www.flaticon.com

Illustrations

Don Hatcher: pages 5 & 16. Simon Kneebone: pages 8 & 22. Angelo Madrid: pages 18 & 21.

Additional acknowledgements

Editorial on behalf of Independence Educational Publishers by Cara Acred.

With thanks to the Independence team: Mary Chapman, Sandra Dennis, Christina Hughes, Jackie Staines and Jan Sunderland.

Cara Acred

Cambridge

May 2016